More or Less
A real life story

Valerie May

Copyright © 2012 Valerie May
All rights reserved.
ISBN: 1975773861
ISBN-13: 9781975773861

DEDICATION

My sincere thanks to the following friends for the love and support over the past years:

Elaine Baxter (deceased)
Jean & David Clements
Jean & David Davies (both deceased)
Barbara Feirek
Alan Large
Nick & Lucy Lang
Dorothy Morgan
Ann Sheppard
Jo Townsend
Dr. H. Yokall

And of course my wonderful and beloved daughter, to whom I have dedicated this book.

VALERIE MAY

CONTENTS

Part 1: Once upon a time   3

Part 2: August 1954–May 1991   29

1963   62

1979, May   86

September 19th, 1979   92

1981   96

1982   102

September, 1982   104

1988   113

1990/1991   118

May 2nd, 1991   121

The Millennium – 2000   137

2003   141

2004   145

2010   150

2011   152

2013   155

Summary   157

Postscript: 2016   158

VALERIE MAY

Part I
Once Upon a Time

This story starts in the middle, has a beginning, sadly no ending – a bizarre story in three parts.

In early May 1991, my husband of thirty-eight years disappeared and has never been found.

We had lived in Somerset three and a half years.

That day began, like any other.

We left home together, we had one car and travelled to the nearby town, which took usually approximately ten to fifteen minutes. My husband asked me, I was driving, to take him to the Crescent car park. He would then walk to the coffee shop he owned and ran, Mondays/Saturday, opening 8:30 a.m. to 6:00 p.m. I was a receptionist in a nearby office, 9:00 a.m. to 4:00 p.m. He got out of the car, did not kiss me, or say farewell, just said we would go for a meal at a public house we went to every Thursday. He did not look back. I waved, but there was no backward glance. I have never seen him since that day.

By the end of that day, I was for a long, long time in a very dark place – due to media attention, banks, building societies, police, people wanting money, always money, very little understanding or compassion, ghoulish interest, theories, it never stopped, after nearly thirty eight years of being married, to someone I began to think I never knew. The evilest thing being the Data Protection Act, who supports the perpetrator, not the sad victim.

I was an only child, born in 1933, late in life to great parents, the best – my dad was a retired policeman and was working for a security company. My mamma, was suffering with very chronic asthma, spent very little time at school, and came from the West Country. My mamma was an absolute whizz, playing poker, any card game and who never lost on the horses, knowing all the form etc. etc. She was naturally funny and although spent a great deal of time indoors, always jolly. She was very pretty, lovely dark auburn curly hair, shapely in a plump way, and wore wonderful hats. My dad was six feet one inch tall, very slim, had china blue eyes, and was very easy to live with. He adored my mother and was always very concerned regarding my mother's health. He was a true Londoner, from Hackney, very funny, never judgemental and wherever he went, everyone liked him. He was wise and most of all, always gave me time. He had the saying, I would rather give you ten minutes than ten bob – something missing in today's society.

My mother was visiting a cousin in London. Her cousin was engaged and brought my dad along to make a foursome, although my mum was engaged to a naval officer, but my parents were married three weeks later on Easter Sunday, quite something in 1927. They were happy for forty eight years, when Alzheimer's took my dear dad away and Mamma died six years later of kidney failure.

I was privately educated, went to a Convent in Ealing W5. I was evacuated in 1940, never spent time away from my home before. We lived in a semi-detached house in Middlesex, good neighbours and community, neat gardens, no one was out of work, mainly the mums stayed at home washing on Mondays, ironing on Tuesdays. Days for baking and keeping their houses clean – no fitted carpets or central heating, fires that made marks on your legs and chilblains on your fingers and toes.

My dad made a little seat in the airing cupboard, so I could dress, leaving my clothes in the cupboard the night before. A real bonus for my mum – a Servis twin tub washing machine. A bike when I passed my scholarship, a birthday party every New Year for my birthday, when my many friends would book every year, as they were so much fun. Only soft drinks, no smoking, just the norm in those days. No violence or vandalism, not that pranks were not played, just great fun.

I went dancing every Saturday at the Town Hall with a real band. Fridays I went to the Church Youth Club, numerous activities were organised, cycling, walking, musical evenings. Many young people played an instrument. I had won a scholarship to the Royal College of Music, when I was eleven and played the piano. Popular at parties and functions, as television was still in its infancy – my dad bought our first TV in 1953 to watch the Coronation and most of the street came to our home to watch. I was very fortunate, as with my dad's police connections I was smuggled into Westminster Abbey to see the greatest of occasions. I don't know if I will live to see another. I have never forgotten that very rainy day. I was twenty years old.

Another day to remember was the V.E. day. My dad took me up to Buckingham Palace and somehow again I got to see everything, as I was hoisted up onto Reuter's stand by Queen Victoria's Statue and looked down on all the happy people. I was twelve years old.

In 1946 my dad was awarded the O.B.E. for his service during the war.

In the main it was given as he saved a lady's life in an air raid. She had been blown by a blast in St Martin's Lane, and was bleeding to death from an artery in her groin. My dad was in the vicinity and he rolled up his socks into a ball and held them on her wound and when rescued by ambulance and taken to hospital, he was commended for his thinking and saving her life. My dad was a very unassuming man, when this happened he only told my mamma and all this event was told much later when we went to Buckingham Palace.

I still wind up, every day, the Goliath Hunter watch his colleagues gave him for his bravery. It hangs on a stand in my lounge. I had it made for the watch, which always reminds me of his outstanding kindness and bravery, which was like a ribbon throughout his life.

The next chapter in my life was overwhelming, happy, more fun, which it had always been. Another man came into my life, who like all boyfriends were compared to my dad.

I cannot recall how often I went to the cinema on a Sunday. A friend asked me if I would accompany her to the Regal Cinema, the matinée, to see a film called 'Sentimental Journey'. Maureen O'Hara and John Payne were the leads and the song was the background theme. I asked my parents if they minded and as always they agreed, in view of the miserable rainy, grey weather. It was ten days before Christmas, 1950 – in a fortnight, I would be eighteen years old.

We sat in the 1/9d's – about fourteen rows from the screen – upstairs 3/6d – it was nearly always 1/9d's, it cost a shilling in the front. There was one B film – Pathé News, excerpts from the next week's programme and then the biggy, 'Sentimental Journey'.

It was about half way through the film, two lads behind us kept making silly remarks about the mushy film. It was. I already had dampened one hankie. I decided to tell them to be quiet and I turned and said exactly that.

"Be quiet. I came to see the film, not listen to your remarks."

I recognised one of the young men. My friend at school, Jennifer, always asked him to her birthday parties. He lived three houses away. She thought he was 'dishy'. He played a mean game of tennis and had qualified for Junior Wimbledon. His parents could not afford any tuition and there were no sponsors at that time. He remarked to his friend that he liked a girl with spunk and lovely smiley blue eyes. He asked me if he could walk me home, but I refused as I was with my friend.

We enjoyed the rest of the film, no more remarks, and left at the end. I never gave it another thought. Unbeknown to me, he went to see Jennifer, asked where I lived, went back to Aldershot Barracks – he was doing his last year in National Service in the R.O.A. – and wrote a letter.

What followed, my dad gave him nine out of ten for cheek, nerve and charm.

He wrote to my dad and it went like this.

He had seen his lovely daughter in the cinema and as it was coming to the season of goodwill, could he come and visit to take me out with mistletoe as a gift.

My dear dad told me he had received a letter, but not the content. On

Christmas Eve, I had gone to midnight service with friends. The doorbell rang – my dad told me this episode afterwards. He was full of Dutch courage and nervous, but asked if I was there. My dad apologised for not replying to his letter, it would have crossed the wire, as he had come home on leave early. He asked if he could come up on Christmas Day, no Boxing Day, no – we had family Christmases. He suggested and said please come, as a reward for perseverance, to Valerie's eighteenth birthday party on the following Saturday, 2nd January, 1951. My dad told me afterwards. I laughed and said we shall see! Secretly I liked him already. I had had boyfriends before, not one who was so cheeky and persistent, and I know my dad had already given him points, on reflection, not unlike himself when he met my mamma, overwhelmed her with love and attention all those years ago, and they lived happily for forty eight years.

On 2nd January, 1951, at seven on the dot, the doorbell rang. I opened the door and there was the young man who had written a letter, spoken to me in a dark cinema thirteen days ago. He was about five feet eleven inches tall, broad-shouldered, narrow waist, knitted red tie, dark trousers. He had very dark brown curly, curly hair (I love curly hair), kind brown eyes, Roman nose, and hands you noticed immediately, tapering fingers with Filbert nails, expressive. He took off his grey gabardine raincoat, smiled and said, "At last". He motioned to me to sit on the bottom of the stairs, gave me a brown package, which when opened contained a box of Black Magic chocolates (I've always liked milk, he didn't know that, did he?) and a 78 rpm record of 'Peanut Vendor' by Stan Kenton. I had never heard of Peanut Vendor, and who was Stan Kenton? I thanked him, suggested he took the record back and if not refundable, I'd rather have 'Fingal's Cave' from the Hebrides Suite or 'Rustle of Spring', which I was trying to master on the piano. He laughed and said he didn't know them either. He liked jazz, swing.

He said, "Are you always this honest and being spunky, like telling me to be quiet in the cinema?"

I in turn laughed and said we'll talk about it later.

I took him in to meet my mum and dad. He was very polite, calling my dad 'Sir', confident and self-assured. Other guests arrived; he knew many of them who had been to the same Grammar School and youth club. He fitted in fine. Never left my side, listening to everything, asking what I liked and disliked, my favourite things. He was attentive and would put his arm around my waist and shoulder, naturally but not intrusively. The evening flew by.

He told me many times how much he liked my blue eyes, whispering voice, in fact he liked just everything about me. It was at this time – I get a buzz in my heart. I'll describe what he liked and saw. I was five feet three inches, small-boned, approximately seven stone, dark, long brown wavy hair, either tied back with a ribbon or in a ponytail. I had small hands and feet, size four, white straight teeth, being a happy person I smiled a lot. I tried to cautiously say what I thought, so as not to hurt feelings – my dad's wise words were: 'It's not what you say, it's the way that you say it'. I was quite a nervous person and although appeared at ease, needed injections of confidence, which after being with this young man in my life, I got better and better.

He had seven more days' leave before returning to Aldershot. He had another twelve months before finishing his National Service. He had built his own bicycle and on a good trip did the journey in just fifty nine minutes, from door to door.

As he left my birthday party, he said, "I'll come back to see you tomorrow and every day after, I'll be here at five-ish".

My mother interrupted and invited him to tea, no doubt to eat the leftovers. I always had a proper birthday cake. My parents were always aware that having a birthday so near Christmas, you missed out – getting combined gifts and birthday cards, forgotten, and being over New Year, I rarely got a card on the right date, as there was no post over New Year's Day, and still do!

When I was born my parents put an announcement in the newspaper. They had been given the best gift ever for New Year 1933. I will relate a funny aside about this time. My mother wanted to call me Geraldine Elizabeth. My dad appeared to agree, but had reservations. It was a long name to spell and a mouthful. I was born at home and therefore my registration was in the Registrar's Office. My dear dad, in the car, debated in his head about my name.

When he got to the Office, he asked the Registrar, "What do you think about Valerie Ann for my new daughter?"

He thought it was very nice, not a name that would date, like Jean, Elsie, etc., so Valerie Ann it was. My dad did not tell my Mum immediately and when I was being perambulated around the park, my parents were stopped by friends, admired the baby and asked my name. Promptly my mother said Geraldine Elizabeth. My dad interrupted and very quietly – no – 'Valerie Ann'. Valerie because we love her and Ann after my wife, her grandmother, great-grandmother. Wow! My Mum was speechless and did not speak to Dad for days, but as always it was reconciled and agreed a good name – and I have always been eternally grateful. Geraldine Elizabeth, no thank you. I was always called Valerie – never Val – and if that did happen, I always rectified same, as did my parents.

As promised, my boyfriend came the next day – by midday I was aware I was going to have a cold. I used to get colds, like no-one else. Days of sneezing, sore nose, cold sores, feeling heavy-headed and flu-like symptoms of lethargy, aching and generally feeling awful and looking like a rag.

I warned him. He was gallant and said he didn't care. Colds pass in nine days; three coming, three here and three going. He had not obviously had colds like mine. I raided my dad's handkerchief drawer, no tissues in shops in those days.

My mid-evening, I was sneezing and dripping non-stop, sore throat, no point in make-up, as constantly wiping it off in damp hankies. Although early days, kissing was out of the question, even a goodnight one. He kept reassuring me, it would pass and I would be my lovely self again and we were going to be together for a long, long time. How could a cold interfere with that?

By the following Friday, symptoms had abated considerably – we went to the cinema – 'The Mudlark', a tale surrounding a street waif who goes into the Palace to see Queen Victoria. He always held my hand wherever and constantly asked if I was okay.

After two more happy days, he returned to camp, promising to write every day. He took a photograph from my parents' mantel shelf, with their permission of course, and said it would be the first thing he would see and last heaven he would see before he went to sleep. Boys don't romance girls anymore – they do not know what they're missing.

He kept his promise. In the early fifties there were three posts a day. I received a letter, sometimes two, at 2½d per letter, by every post – 8:00 a.m., noon and 4:00 p.m. I would read my 8:00 a.m. on the train to Baker Street. My Mum would telephone and say another had arrived at noon. I had two to three letters to read on my evening return home at 6:40 p.m.

He came home most weekends – Friday to Sunday. He left camp at five-ish, home, bathed and something to eat and on my doorstep by 7:00 p.m. He always bought me a gift, not important to the world, very important to me – flowers – a rose, my favourite – always pale pink, silver thimble, records (not Stan Kenton). I had great admiration for Nat King Cole alongside my classic 'Unforgettable', 'Autumn Leaves', and many more. Poetry books, a lovely lace handkerchief, pair of nylons which were scarce. Such a treat and lasted much longer than silk, and only worn on special occasions. Always in ribboned containers, which I cherished so much.

Our favourite song was 'September Song', sung by Walter Huston from a film 'Knickerbocker Holiday'. Of course, I had the record.

He was tender, tactile and oh so loving. Every time he came in the room, a button was pressed in my heart and this wonderful feeling spilled everywhere. I called it my 'buzz button'. It never went away, but sadly lays dormant beside the ache I always feel, now he is no longer with me.

Although Capricorns are down-to-earth, conservative people, we are incurably romantic. I loved how he must think of me and I was overwhelmed that someone other than my parents could love me so much.

It was sweet, mysterious and wonderful.

During the year of 1951, I really had a great time, both in my job and personally. I worked in a theatre agency called Webster & Girling in Baker Street, near the Abbey National building, with a clock as big as Big Ben. Keith Prowse was the largest agency, we were second. I was a Shorthand Typist and had a tiny office in the basement. Also I was a 'go for' for all the staff, mostly male. They treated me so well, being married with daughters the same age – never demanding and treating me like a lady. One of the great perks of the position was 'free theatre tickets', so the front desk would promote shows to customers. London was beginning to have great theatre – stars from the USA, Laurence Olivier and Vivien Leigh, Ralph Richardson, John Gielgud, Edith Evans, a young Richard Attenborough, Michael Redgrave, Dirk Bogarde, and so many others. The Rodgers & Hammerstein musicals, Lerner & Loewe, I saw them all, as tickets were shared around the staff.

In the next paragraphs, I'll list as many as I can.

Frank Sinatra, Nat King Cole, Danny Kaye, Billy Eckstine, Vic Damone, Dean Martin and Jerry Lewis, Bob Hope, Mel Tormé, Billy Daniels, Sammy Davis Jr., Lew Rawls, Gracie Allen and George Burns, Sarah Vaughan, Ella Fitzgerald, Lena Horne – a stunning lady, very elegant and beautiful. The Andrews Sisters, Beverley Sisters, Vera Lynn, Anne Shelton. On one occasion Sarah Vaughan duetted with Billy Eckstine on 'Ev'ry Time We Say Goodbye, I Cry a Little'. It was magic. Later, they made it into a single disc. I played it endlessly. The London Palladium was the mecca of big stars and all musical greats appeared there.

I also went to plays, comedies – 'Caesar and Cleopatra', and on alternative weeks 'Antony and Cleopatra' at the Haymarket. The Oliviers were the King and Queen of theatre.

'The Moon & Sixpence', 'The Mousetrap'. The theatre I enjoyed most of all was my season ticket for the 'The Proms' that my dad bought me every year and musicals never before seen in London. Royal Drury Lane was the theatre. It has the biggest stage in London with a huge revolving stage.

I went to the first night of 'Oklahoma'. 'Curly' was played by Harold Keel, who when he went to Hollywood changed his name to Howard. I was in a box level with the stage and when he came out singing 'Oh What a Beautiful Morning', I was mesmerised. He was so handsome and manly. I saw it eleven more times and threw carnations on the stage. I knew all of the songs and drove my boyfriend and my parents mad, constantly playing it on my record player.

'Carousel' for me was a more serious musical. Bill Johnson, another American baritone, played the lead. His soliloquy had great lyrics and melody and was the first song spoken with the theme in the background. It lasted nearly fifteen minutes. Lovely songs – '(When I Marry) Mr Snow' – I could go on and on.

'The Pajama Game' was another favourite. The love song 'Hey There, You with the Stars in Your Eyes'. My parents' sitting room housed all the records I just had to have. When I was twenty one, my parents bought me an electric Ferguson console record player. No more winding up by hand, I was so fortunate to have generous parents.

I saw 'Kismet', the main song 'Strangers in Paradise' and the music of Borodin adapted. It was lovely to look at, being set in an Arabian Nights background. When my boyfriend came home, I used to regale him with my outings and re-enact the songs and play them both on the piano and records.

During that year, I had several exciting and unexpected happenings.

My boss, Mr Wallis, called me into his office one day and asked me to go to the Washington Hotel in Mayfair. The Washington, like its name, was American and many USA stars stayed there. I had to deliver some theatre tickets, collect payment and return to Baker Street. I used to walk everywhere. I knew London like the back of my hand. Besides, buses were crowded and cost valuable threepenny pieces.

I had never been to the hotel before. The reception area was very grand in modern décor, very smart dark green walls and cream furniture and fittings, flowers everywhere. I gave the receptionist the ticket envelope, presumed the tickets would be delivered, checked and the cheque or money given, and I would return to Baker Street.

The receptionist spoke on the telephone. "Please go up to the suite, you are invited for tea."

This was a first. The door was opened by a maid and I was ushered into a type of salon; sofas, soft lights and very special. Through the door came Elizabeth Taylor. She was stunning. About as tall as myself, violet eyes and eyelashes to die for; they were not artificial. She was rather short of leg, very beautiful, really breathtaking. She was so kind, told me to sit down and put me at ease. Tea and chocolate cake was brought in on a trolley, and we were joined by Mike Todd. They had been married very recently and were on their way home to the USA

I felt I was outside my body – having tea and cake with Elizabeth Taylor. I stayed nearly three quarters of an hour. Miss Taylor asked me my name, where I lived, about my boyfriend. I said I enjoyed so much the theatre, music and the film she made with Montgomery Clift – 'A Place in the Sun'. She thanked me and said Montgomery and her were very good friends and she would tell him. She gave me the payment for the theatre tickets, they were going that evening with friends. On leaving, my feet were not touching the ground. It was raining hard. Miss Taylor asked how I came. I replied – walked. "My goodness, we can't have that," and promptly called reception and ordered their car to take me back to Baker Street. I protested, she insisted. In a way, I was disappointed as I was intending to stop at least two people in the street and say, "Guess what? I've had tea with Elizabeth Taylor and Mike Todd!"

On jumping out of the Rolls Royce, with thanks, I ran into the office, called everyone to attention, related my story. They all smiled and said 'well done' and went back to the job in hand. I said, "Don't you think it's exciting?" I was so disappointed.

Why is it, as you age, thrills and excitement slip away. Does it go into the misty corners of your mind? Is it one of those unanswerable questions, like children ask and adults cannot answer? My mother said I asked very often when I was young, "Where does the wool go when you get a hole in your sock? Why isn't it in a neat pile in your shoe?" She would always laugh and say, "I don't know". Life is full of unanswerables, I guess. When my boyfriend came home, of course, I told him. He was impressed, as he always was and that's all that mattered because I loved him so.

In April 1951, my boyfriend wrote in one of his many letters, he would take me out for a meal on the following Saturday. He wanted to tell me something and ask me another. I was intrigued, nervous, but had no qualms. We rarely went out to a restaurant, as it was expensive. He wanted some quiet and just us together. What follows is I think very sad, understandable as the story was not acceptable by narrow-minded people, or society on the whole; the middle classes could be very bigoted – all classes for that matter.

My boyfriend:

My parents are not my birth parents.

Christmas 1930. The person you know and I call Mother, her younger sister of seventeen, came to stay over the holiday. Also, my father's younger brother was also invited. Obviously, over Christmas the younger folk got it together and I am the outcome. For the families, thrown into turmoil and the stigma that went with this happening. The situation was addressed by the people he called Mum and Dad – who were childless and living away from Wales where they all came from – adopted me. There was no legal work and I have a shortened birth certificate and neither of my natural parents were named.

He was born late in the following September 1931.

Now, in this day and age, you could say, what a great result. Then eighteen months later they had their own son and my loved one took second place. Never any birthday cards, not even on his twenty-first, and emotionally neglected.

They never discussed it and this I feel is the saddest thing, never told him. When he was sixteen, the Grammar School he attended was organising foreign holidays. There were forms to be completed and his Headmaster called him in and said: "Your parents have disclosed that you are not their natural son, not legally adopted either." This was a revelation, especially as his parents had asked the Headmaster to tell him this news. Evidently, he did not leave his room for two days. His parents never apologised and just pushed the issue under the carpet and this lasted always. He never appeared to resent this sadness, but later in life, one evening when he had a few whiskeys, it came to the surface.

"Valerie, you don't realise what it's like to be rejected and feel unloved," and, of course, I could not respond, as my background was just the opposite.

He held my hand across the table and said, "You are the first person I have told and please assure me it makes no difference to us and what I feel for you".

I reassured him ardently. How could it make a difference? If he had not been honest, I would be none the wiser and I thanked him profusely for being honest. Whatever had happened to him, I loved him so much. No event would ever make any difference.

"What will your parents think?" he asked and I again reassured him they would be fine, because of the people they were.

I said, "Now what is the second thing you wanted to say?"

"Valerie, darling, you are my girl forever and always. Please say you will marry me."

I really don't have to say my reply. Of course it was yes and I jumped up and to all the people's amazement in the restaurant, kissed him. I don't know how many times. He smiled and smiled and I hoped all the previous unhappy conversation faded away.

I told my parents what had transpired and of course all was well. My mamma said he was a 'gem', my dad 'a gentleman', and I just loved him to the moon and back.

My boyfriend said he would ask my dad's permission the following weekend and said think what kind of engagement ring you would like. We decided to get officially engaged on the date we were first together – my birthday. So 2nd January, 1952, was the date. I would be nineteen years old.

If this account of my life is ever in print, please recollect what has been said about the beginnings of my husband's life. I feel it is very relevant to what happened and how he reacted and behaved later on, when events went wrong. Sins of the father etc. etc. He was being punished, he thought.

I realise in the 1950s when I became aware, a great deal of life was about sinning. Reasons were never addressed, too strict parents, the church and snobbery.

Abortion, illegitimacy, people living together, stillborn babies and sex were never talked about. All taboo subjects and if you did talk about it, you were considered promiscuous and not nice to know. Now the pendulum has swung way to the other side. I'd like it to swing a little way back, especially with the foul language, our beautiful language so desecrated and the word is never relevant to the phrase or sentence. Mary Whitehouse would spin in her grave.

A funny aside – I had been told I could ask anything by my parents, and I did!

I came home from the office one day and at the dinner table asked, "What is a thespian?"

My dad said, "What do you think it is?"

I thought it was maybe another word for lesbian. My dad fell about and explained it was someone who trod the boards, an actor and such like. I was quite disappointed, as I was sure it was a rude word.

The following Saturday duly arrived.

My boyfriend was there on time as usual. I had mentioned to my dad that he wanted to speak to him. They went in the other room, the sitting room, never heard of lounges in those days, a posher word, I expect people thought later.

I heard them talking and laughing, all smiles – my dad was delighted and said he was like the son he never had and my mamma was very pleased too. He said call us Pops and Mum from now on.

Of course, like all girls, I did think about my engagement ring. I would like a sapphire with diamonds, like a flower in platinum, not gold, which was unusual in those days.

A great friend of my parents, who I had always called Uncle, was a gemologist and bought precious stones for Watches of Switzerland. They had many outlets and he worked from their Ludgate Circus branch. He was given the Freedom of London, which was a great honour. When he heard about my engagement, offered to obtain some stones and have it made for me in Hatton Garden.

He talked to me at length and said sapphires were not easily obtainable and that solitaires, three stone and five stone diamonds, were more valuable and modern. My mother had a five stone diamond ring.

No sapphires were forthcoming. One evening he brought a lovely solitaire with diamond shoulders set in platinum and I decided – my fiancé promised me a sapphire ring one day and he as always kept his promise. When we were married, I had a lovely orange blossom platinum wedding ring to complete the set.

In later years, I had my ring set in my mother's wedding ring, with initials of both my parents and ours.

My fiancé kept my ring in his mother's pantry in a sugar bowl and I used to wear it every time I visited until my birthday in 1952, as arranged the eight months before. He thought I was a funny girl and always surprising him.

With my parents' approval, we would get married sometime in 1954. I would be twenty one years old and my fiancé twenty two, nearly twenty three.

In 1952 my fiancé came out of his National Service in late January. For a brief time he had worked at the Middlesex County Council, did not enjoy and after discussion with me, he had decided to take exams in Customs & Excise and look to being a Customs Officer. Heathrow Airport was becoming a major airport and he saw a future maybe there. He went back to the M.C.C. and went to night school. The course was two years for Customs & Excise late in 1952. Again, some friends of my parents, they played 'Solo' every Friday. Uncle Albert and Auntie Waddy, they had one son, George. George had a position at Unilever. He wanted my fiancé to know that vacancies were available and he thought he may be interested. Salaries were much better than the M.C.C. and may tide him over until he had got his exams. The long and short of it – my fiancé had a series of interviews and was accepted with flying colours and went to 'Pepsodent', one of their companies, in selling.

He liked it very much, made many friends. Went from strength to strength. He rowed for Unilever in the Head of the River race, held a week after Oxford and Cambridge boat race. He also won several prizes for skulling. I was always concerned, as he was not a good swimmer, and I was frightened he may fall in. He allayed my fears with a kiss and a cuddle and said nothing could happen when he had a girl like me to love. When you are in love, anything is possible. You do get older and wiser, sadly.

In 1952, the King, George VI, died and there was great expectancy having a young queen and great plans for the Coronation in 1953. The war was not talked about and remembered so much. We were nearly free of clothing coupons and rationing. London was being rebuilt and generally everyone felt uplifted and more prosperous.

The year flew by. My fiancé and I were very happy and had so many plans, mainly to have a home of our own. He passed his exams with merit. Unilever were starting a new company – Birds Eye Frozen Foods. Clarence Birdseye was a Canadian and thought up the notion of quick freezing vegetables and packaging and selling from frozen food refrigerators – a new and original concept.

They were looking for representatives to go to retail outlets to sell the product to the public. As all who read this know, what a success it was, and still is.

My fiancé opted to stay on with the company and rapidly became one of their salesmen. In fact, his mother said he did the costs in his sleep and everything revolved around frozen peas, a vegetable I've never liked very much. There were other things that occupied us, like necking and thinking about being married.

MORE OR LESS

In the spring of 1953, my fiancé asked me if I thought my parents would allow us to go on holiday together. My parents as always were fine, said they know they could trust us both.

We decided not to go far from London. Margate was the destination. I had never been anywhere except the West Country to my nan's in Devon. I was evacuated for a short time near Cullompton to a lady who had a smallholding, was not married, therefore no children. She was very kind, but no clues regarding children's needs.

My parents kept a letter I wrote at that time in their wallet – asking:

Please may I come home, as Miss Davis gives me stewed apples on Monday, baked apple on Tuesday, apple crumble on Wednesdays and then it starts all over again. If you don't come and fetch me, I'm going to die of apple poisoning.

Of course, my parents did come for me and said we would take our chances in the capital and the Blitz – I have never eaten apples since.

Our friends were very envious and amazed we were going on holiday and their parents were more than surprised at my parents. All was well, we had a great time, good weather and the accommodation a Victorian house, very narrow, dining room overlooking the street and the sea across the road.

We found it very amusing. The landlady put me in a room at the back of the dining room, woke me up every morning – throwing the cutlery on the table. Everyone sat together on a trestle table. My fiancé was on the top floor, front. I'm sure she fancied him as every morning he got a cup of tea, was brought in hot water for shaving, and sat on the bed and watched. The food was very good with good company thrown in.

Uppermost in our minds was saving money for a deposit. Renting was very hard; landlords asked for key money and it was usually six months' rental in advance. The flats we did view were either one large room, grubby, inadequate washing facilities, noisy. We were offered a flat over an undertakers, the entrance through the chapel of rest. My fiancé wasn't bothered, but I felt our friends would be inhibited with the occupants! Although they would be quiet.

Another amusing experience – a basement flat in Notting Hill. Again, a Victorian house. The agent showed us into a very small hall, no lighting, the landlord could not afford rewiring. It was dangerous to use the switches.

We were shown into a lounge/dining room. It had a paraffin lamp on a low table, very dark – we became aware of light fluffing noises and squeaks. There were small birds flying around and defecating on the walls and lovely coving. On the mantel shelf a well-known marmalade jar full of bird seed and a bigger one on the other end full of condoms, or French Letters as they were called then. The bedroom was miniscule – it would have been an obstacle race to get into bed!

We thanked the agent, but no thank you.

On returning home, when I told my parents, my dear dad laughed, couldn't believe it. My mamma was disgusted, especially when I told about the mantelpiece ornaments. You never spoke of things like that. I said maybe they passed them around to guests 'like After Eights'. My mother was not amused.

We became very despondent and wondered what we could do.

My dad came to our rescue and I will tell you later.

In late 1953, my mamma did improve in health. She had new medication. There were tests at St Mary's Hospital, Paddington, for allergies. It was found she had nine serious ones. Generally, she was much more buoyant and even went on a short holiday with my dad to Great Yarmouth, chosen because it was so flat and would not exert her breathing. The downside was she was diagnosed with emphysema in her lungs. It caused great foreboding for her friends and family. She always took it in her stride and was optimistic, as we were also, for her benefit and morale.

I remember very vividly when I was ten years old, during the war, my dad woke me up in the early hours, put my dressing gown on, told me to keep my head down and go to our doctor's home. Mamma had overdosed on her adrenaline during an attack and needed his help. I was frightened running through the night. My dad told me to be brave and run like the wind. I banged on Doctor David's door, lights went on, he appeared in his dressing gown. I gasped what Dad had said. He picked up his case, shut the door after shouting to his wife, held my hand tightly and we ran home. He stayed with my mother until 7:00 a.m.

My dad and I sat on the stairs – he assured Daddy Mamma would be okay. He gave me 2/6d for being a brave girl and said you deserve a medal. My dad bought me a book I wanted and put a special inscription inside. That does not happen anymore.

Next is what happened re. our future home living situation after we were married.

One evening my parents asked my fiancé and I to sit around the dining table, suggesting we discuss an idea they had thought over very seriously.

My parents said they realised there seemed very little hope for us finding a home. They suggested that they would be wiling for us to live with them. We could save money, they would allow us to stay, without any payment. My dad said if we could save £500 he would double it, which opens the door to having a mortgage and a home of our own. We all agreed, thought in depth must be given and we would talk again in a week's time.

We decided to both write down the pros and cons and come together and discuss our lists before our proposed next meeting.

For us both, saving money as quickly as possible was the ultimate paramount. My fiancé would get a salary increase on a regular basis – I, of course, would ask for a rise. My company was mean in outlook. I received £5 per week being a Shorthand Typist and no vision of being a secretary, a coveted position, and there was only one, the Chairman's. I had to cover my rail season ticket, clothes and payment to my parents, never regular holidays, like we have today.

The main disadvantage, which was important then and still is, was having time and space together without other people giving their well-meaning advice, views etc. Communication between just you and your husband/wife, always someone listening in and giving their opinions and views.

I was reluctant in another area – we would not have our things, wedding gifts, furniture. It would be just my new husband moving in, very little privacy. My dear dad, as always, helped that situation, promising they would go to the cinema one evening and play cards another evening, two nights out of seven to be alone. My fiancé was very sympathetic, but always in our minds, saving money was the ultimate. This was a grand and generous offer by my parents and we decided to grasp the nettle.

My fiancé had no qualms that life would be tranquil. He got on so well with my parents. I was the more volatile and impatient in getting our own home. Could not come quick enough. I wanted the time to fly by. My fiancé decided to take on two extra jobs, as a barman in a public house two nights a week and worked in a tailors on Saturdays, taking exams and Birds Eye as well. I knew throughout these writings, I reiterate, young people, not generalising, just don't have that get up and go. They want cars, flats and material things without doing very little, just expect it to materialise or else whinge and do not apply themselves.

When we came together again, we gave our concerns. All agreed it would be the quickest way through to our aim. As you will read, it did happen and all was well.

Our friends thought we were very brave and many shook their heads in disbelief that it just would not work!

I give a chapter to another happening – I did not foresee, it also taught me a valuable lesson.

My fiancé was always loving and when he did not see me through working, would write a letter full of love and dreams. In the year after we met, his last year in National Service, I received 947 letters, kept in date order in a shoe box. They were added to by cards, notes, birthday and anniversary cards. I kept them until 2006, fifty five years. I read them many, many times, remembering, wishing for all that love to come back again.

I have kept six or seven of his letters. I chose at random. I was advised to destroy them, as it may help with healing my grief – it did not. I have a very good memory. They are embedded in my heart and mind and belong only to me. People are well-meaning, but always follow your heart, as long as it does not hurt anyone else.

I am taking another go at putting pen to paper on my first sentence, re. an unforeseen event and the lesson learnt.

In March 1954, I was having my breakfast. Always two pieces of toast and lemon curd and a very hot cup of tea – I still do – boring, yes, I just like.

Mamma was reading a letter, which after a few minutes was folded and returned to its envelope. She then turned to me and said, "Valerie, you cannot be married on June 30th".

I had always wanted to be married in June; roses, long evenings, warm weather, a romantic notion maybe, not something out of the ordinary, I think you will agree.

I knew I had heard what she said, then it made an impact. I repeated her announcement and then it made another impact – why, Mamma? Explain.

My mother's youngest sister Dorothy and her husband with his job had gone to Gibraltar for two years previously and were not returning until August. I, of course, presumed they would come over in June for my wedding. My mother in turn said I should wait, only another seven weeks, so that they could attend and I was also reminded, Auntie Dot, as she was called, was my Godmother and wanted to be there.

I left for Baker Street with mixed feelings, resentment, then reconciled my thoughts that my fiancé wouldn't mind! We had booked our honeymoon, at least my fiancé had, cars were booked and the venue decided. I had bought material for my bridesmaids, my two best friends, Pamela and Dorothy. All day I rehearsed what I was going to tell my fiancé. I could not talk to my biggest ally, my dad, as he had left before the post arrived. My mother had decided. In hindsight, thank goodness, my dad had not had the invitations printed!

It never occurred to me to telephone my fiancé. That was my first error. I just presumed he would agree. It was a Thursday, one of the evenings my parents were at the cinema.

My fiancé arrived as they left. We went to the sitting room, cuddled up on the settee and then I made my announcement.

"We cannot be married in June. Mamma's sister is coming back in August, so it will have to be arranged around that."

My fiancé put me at arm's length, said, "So that is it? I am not to be consulted? I am not marrying your auntie and are you always going to do as your mother decides without at least talking first?"

I, in turn, took the stance: "You are being silly, and another seven weeks isn't the end of the world. If you can't wait, then perhaps we should not get married at all!"

He said, "It's not that issue, it's just that you have given me an ultimatum without any thought to my feelings. You have, in fact, given an order and that's not fair."

I said, "I think you should leave. As far as I am concerned, it's fine. Obviously, you have other ideas."

I fully expected him to say Valerie, of course I'll marry you, any date, whatever. He did leave without saying anything.

I ran upstairs in floods of tears into my parents' front bedroom, sure he would see me and come back. He did not and disappeared into the nearby station. I was furious and in anger, threw my engagement ring out of the window. I went in my own room and between sobbing and saying to myself I did not care and wish I'd never known him.

My parents arrived home to find me distraught, annoyed, and very red-eyed. My mum didn't know what all the fuss was about and said my fiancé was being unreasonable. Whereas my dad, the wise, agreed my fiancé had a point and I should not have decided on his part, equally he told me he was, knowing my fiancé it could be resolved. I was sure it was all over, did not sleep, fighting my emotions and yet trying not to give in, that I had made a booboo, and I was the one who was being unreasonable.

I woke up on Friday, told my mum I was not going to Baker Street today and promptly went into Harrow and bought a pair of shoes I could not afford and all the time talking to myself, sometimes out loud. Was I at fault? My fiancé was being difficult, behaviour I had not seen before. He was always understanding. No doubt he had had a bad day and was being irrational. I just wasn't having it. Perhaps that spunk he admired in me was going to be my downfall.

I overheard my dad say, "Goodness, Etty," (short for Ethel), "have you forgotten what it's like to be in love? As soon as I saw you, three weeks seemed like an eternity. Valerie and her fiancé have been engaged two and a half years. He is young and healthy and loves our precious daughter so much. I admire he's waited this time".

I heard no comment from Mamma.

During this day, Friday, my fiancé had gone to see my uncle, the gentleman who had been involved re. my engagement ring. He was staying with my parents at this time. My fiancé said how is at number eighty two? My uncle suggested a milk box of chocolates and a record. My favourite at that time was Billy Eckstine. As always my fiancé's initiative came into play and bought Billy singing 'I Apologise' and with this ammunition arrived early evening at my home. By the by, I told my parents my ring was in the garden. I was still so rattled, I had not gone out to look for it.

My dad answered the door, left my fiancé at the door. I was sitting on the settee. Once again, I looked like a rag, full of defiance. As soon as I saw him he smiled, I smiled, and in unison we said sorry. I blamed me profusely.

He said, "Let me explain why I was so upset. Of course, I'll marry you on any date, in any month. I was just annoyed you told me, did not ask if it was okay. We must make decisions together, not presume what someone decides you must automatically obey without considering other people's feelings."

He was, of course, quite right. He went on to say he understood my mother's thoughts, nevertheless I must think for myself. Loads of kisses, all was forgiven – we went in to see my parents with diaries at the ready, the date set Saturday 14th August at 2:00 p.m., St John's Church. I whispered to my dad to get those invitations sorted in case Mamma changed it again. A smile from my dad said it all. He was going to be the beloved father of the bride. I realised how important he was in my life and I had been blessed with someone very like him. I know how very disappointed he would have been what happened in the far away days. He just would not have understood for the first time in his life.

To continue and conclude this incident, with all the apologies, a new date for our nuptials, clean out of my head – my ring!

"You are going to be angry all over again!" I burst into tears.

My fiancé, his arm around me, said, "What's wrong?"

"I threw my ring out of the window in temper last evening."

"Never mind. When I can afford it, I'll buy you that sapphire."

He suggested that tomorrow he would come early and find it. After all, it did not have legs and must be there. My dad was not working, so volunteered as well. Once again I was very restless this night. Very relieved my fiancé and I were back on track, madly in love and definite date set.

By lunchtime still no ring. I stood in the bedroom and did a demonstration and then reconstruction to no avail, and daft really, as I was before not behaving and no doubt a great deal more force and temper was in place the previous evening.

We had lunch. I was reconciled to never seeing my ring again. What an explanation I would have to give. They would think I was going bananas. Unlike me, my fiancé and dad didn't give up and eureka, Daddy fount it on a standard rose bush just under the window. I danced around to 'I'm in Love with a Wonderful Guy'. I knew every song from South Pacific. I promised never to take it off again.

In April, I went with the dressmaker to London to decide on material for my wedding dress. Mrs Wallis was the wife of my boss at Baker Street. She had trained at Harvey Nichols in Knightsbridge and had made several evening dresses for me over my teens and generously was making my dress as a gift. My bridesmaids' material was printed silk organza, white, over taffeta dresses of lilac, sleeveless, wearing long lilac gloves with coronets of freesia, in those lovely colours, pink/cream/lilac, like sugared almond colours. They were both five feet six inches with dark curly hair and very pretty as well. Dorothy, a year younger than me, attended the same

Grammar School as my fiancé, so were friends. Pamela and I had known each other from way back. She lived in Hampshire. Her mother had gone to school and lived in the same road in Plymouth as my mamma. Pam's dad was in the navy and had been killed during the war. We were great buddies and like me Pam loved musicals and romantic films and at every opportunity she would come up to London on the coach, the cheapest way to travel. When I had extra tickets for a show, I spent many happy times with Pamela and wanted her near on my special day.

Mrs Wallis knew all the places to go. Material was not long after coupons, so we could indulge. I had a definite idea, but not much vision and in hindsight would have done one or two things differently. I chose yards of Nottingham lace to go over three organza slips, cut on the bias. The pattern had a scalloped hem going into a short train, fifty rouleau buttons for interest down the back. What I liked most of all was a cathedral length veil I bought on my own one Saturday, just idling with ideas. It was beautiful, very fine and around the border tiny seed pearls. I knew I'd feel like a princess.

My fiancé was buying the flowers, so told me to have exactly what I wanted. I chose a coronet of orange blossom and of course my bouquet was pale pink, creamy roses and lily of the valley, in a crescent shape. I could not have anything too overpowering, as I was still only just seven stone. I will relate more about our day in a later chapter.

My fiancé described me to his friends. I was his pocket Venus. Very flattering, except I did have arms! And I hoped I was never cold like marble. He agreed. We were both very tactile. I just loved his curly hair and expressive hands. He was the best looking boy on the block. All my friends thought so. Wasn't I lucky.

April went into May, past our former wedding date. My auntie was returning from Gibraltar on 9th August, plenty of time before the 14th. My fiancé was able to change the honeymoon date, cars and photographer in place. The vicar was going to be away. Instead, we had a Monsieur Sabourin, a French young man, although he had a very definite accent. As long as he knew how to marry us, it wasn't too important. As it turned out he was charming and kissed me on both cheeks after we said our vows. I was impressed – my mamma thought it wasn't necessary, but I liked it. It was as if he had given his approval. Some vicars are very starchy. Rowan Atkinson was a great vicar in 'Four Weddings and a Funeral'. Believe me, I don't want to knock the seriousness of the occasion, just a little light relief helps with the nerves.

I was the first person to marry in Webster & Girling. I had been spoilt by the older staff and had now graduated to Shorthand Typist to the manager and his deputy. I went out to collect monies from the kiosk at the Cumberland Hotel and many times ambled down Oxford Street with a body bag with £800. In my dreams I ordered furniture, curtains in John Lewis, and many more other goodies. Neither my boss or myself were ever concerned at holding that amount of money. Not today, I think.

One evening I came home from a different tube station, Piccadilly Circus. As I got onto the escalator, I glanced at my shoes and tucked down between the handrail and moving staircase, I spied a leather black wallet. I pulled it out, proceeded to the bottom, moved to one side and looked inside for the owner's name.

In those days, unlike today, if you gave it in to the police and it was not claimed, that was it. I really don't know what happened to it.

I went back up the escalator, telephoned my home. Dad was home and I asked him what I should do. Inside was a card with presumably the owner's name and address. My dad said I was to take it to his home, ask for identification and return same. I gathered the person was a bookmaker and no doubt these fine tissue paper £20 notes were his takings.

He lived at the end of the Piccadilly Line, well nearly, Turnpike Lane. I would not be home for hours. It had to be done, so off I went. There was £800.

After arriving at my destination, it took me twenty five minutes after numerous enquiries to find the street and the house number. I nervously knocked on the door. A man appeared in a mucky vest and trousers that had seen better days. I mentioned tentatively I may have something that belonged to him. May I see a letter or a bill? He was very quick off the mark, mumbling I had interrupted his meal. I confirmed everything was in order and promptly gave him the wallet. He closed the door without any thanks, did not ask any details. I stood outside the house for a full five minutes, disgusted, surprised at his abysmal bad manners. My dad was furious.

He said, "Valerie, you should have taken £20 for your expenses, time and energy and most of all, your honesty."

He did not count the money. People wonder why there is no honesty. With people like that, it comes as no surprise it is very thin on the ground. Kindness and honesty should always be rewarded. I never got home until 9:35 p.m. with not a very good view about the human race.

In my time I have found a gold watch in Wigmore Street, a ruby and diamond ring in a biscuit tin, always handed them in, never received a thank you. Hey ho, what a life.

My fiancé went off to Catterick to do his compulsory fourteen days in the T.A. This happened when you had done National Service and continued for two years. As always he wrote to me twice a day, could not wait to come home. He did not like the regime or wearing an ill-fitting uniform. Our wedding invitations were posted and our banns had to be called in three churches, as we were being married out of our parishes. I had opted for the church where my fiancé and I went to the youth club and all our friends worshipped. We took it in turns to listen and it seemed strange to hear your name called and hopefully no one would object. Ha ha. My future in-laws were asked their views re. the occasion, but did not get involved in anything, always being nervous when family were involved. They were kind people, but had no confidence and I never heard any terms of endearment. I don't think they were very happy, just tolerated each other and life in general. So different to my background.

Webster & Girling gave me as a wedding present a lovely gilt bedroom clock. It came from Mappin & Webb in Lower Regent Street. I was so pleased and thanked everyone individually and also wrote a card. My fiancé and I had some great gifts. My auntie, the Gibraltar one, gave us a Lloyd Loom chair. Now my daughter has it in her guest bedroom. I believe they are a collector's item now, fifty six years later. An ironing board and iron (which I still use) from Unilever Rowing Club, eiderdown and bedspread from my dad's friends at work, Wedgewood biscuit barrel, that disappeared in one of our many moves, along with a box of my shoes! My nan gave me silver teaspoons and cake knives, a dear friend of my mother's gave a breakfast set and many more very important gifts. My parents gave us money, my fiancé's parents some tea/coffee/sugar canisters.

On the day, when they arrived at the church, they asked my fiancé to go across the road to send us a telegram of congratulations. Even on that special day, they could not do it on their own.

Then came the day, Saturday 14th August, 1954. Valerie and her fiancé being married at 2:00 p.m., St John's Church, Wembley. We had been together three years, eight months and twelve days.

The previous day, Pamela and I had our hair done at Harvey Nichols and lunch after at The Roof Restaurant at Derry & Tom's, Knightsbridge, made a last check on dresses, packed my case for my honeymoon, did not eat very much, the story of my life. When I was young, thought food a waste of playtime and in later years, busy, busy, listening to music, dancing, reading, writing a diary every day and enjoying life.

Mr dad brought me breakfast in bed. My usual toast and lemon curd and tea and a very small brandy for nerves. I cannot remember if there were weather forecasts for each day, as we do now. It was the sunniest day, only blue skies and was later recorded as one of the hottest days of the year – in the eighties.

My lovely dad sat on the bed and said he was losing his best girl today and gave me £100. I protested – he explained it was my 'runaway money', to be kept if my fiancé ever hurt me or made me unhappy. I was very close to tears. He realised and said no weeping today, only smiles. He told me to hurry up, as there would be a queue for the bathroom.

My nan was staying with us for the occasion. Pamela, next door.

Dorothy lived a road away and would be around soon, and other family and friends arriving, and guests would go to the church direct. My fiancé rang me and said he was so looking forward to seeing me at 2:00 p.m. and was I happy.

He did not have a stag night; he went out to the Chinese Garden Restaurant in Piccadilly with his best man who was his school friend. Was very interested in unions and Socialism. He had the same surname as my fiancé. Many thought he was his brother. He had really fair curly hair, a complete contrast to my fiancé. He had stayed at Middlesex County Council. My fiancé's brother was now in the Merchant Navy and was away in Australia.

Mamma, at about 11:30 a.m., asked me to go around to the corner shop for a loaf of bread for sandwiches, a snack to tide us over until our reception.

Pamela came too.

We took our time and one neighbour shouted, "Aren't you getting married today, Valerie?"

I nodded and said don't worry, all is well, there's plenty of time. Everything seemed calm at number eighty two. My mamma was determined not to have an asthma attack and fortified herself with sips of brandy.

Pam, Dorothy and I went upstairs. We had taken over my parents' bedroom. The flowers arrived and were placed on the hallstand, where it was cool. Mummy and Daddy in my bedroom.

Mamma had bought a light navy crêpe dress and jacket and the prettiest hat. She looked so good in hats – it was the softest pink dull satin in the shape of a crescent, falling gently over one ear with a fine veil that just touched her temple. Her curly hair was now turning to silver and very attractive. The picture was completed with navy shoes, handbag and gloves. A very elegant feature was a silver fox fur, with lilac heather pinned which Mum placed high over her arm. My dad looked smashing in a navy blue double-breasted suit, a silvery pink tie and a rosebud buttonhole. My dad had never lost his hair or colour. It was Brylcreemed, as was the fashion, and always his lovely china blue, kind eyes, smiling. I gave them both a hug and said super-duper.

Pamela and Dorothy donned their dresses. They were so pretty. Freesia coronets, long gloves, white and lilac looked so fresh on this sunny day.

They helped me do up my rouleau buttons, six on each sleeve, my three slips making it billow around me. I had three blue bows sewn into the hem of my lace dress, a lace handkerchief of my nan's pinned to my waist, a pair of calf leather white sandals I had worn three years before as a bridesmaid to a second cousin, and something new, I thought, my new husband, therefore abiding by the saying 'Something old, something new, something borrowed, something blue'.

The car arrived. Mummy, Dorothy and Pamela left and also my nan, leaving Daddy and I alone.

We sat on the bottom of the stairs, with my dress laid up the stairs. My dad held my hand and told me how always he was proud of me and how much joy I had brought into his and Mummy's life.

The car returned, I picked up my rose bouquet and we left for St John's. We went by Rolls Royce. Usually it's the first journey in such a great car. You don't know about the second time, when complete silence and sleep comes to your life.

I made sure I enjoyed it and waved and smiled to all and sundry on my way.

The church was at the lower end of the high street, the shops started about seventy five yards along. It was very old, traditional, with a lych gate with a seat on either side. Very old graves sinking into the ground. No one had been buried there for years. Cremation was now an option and was becoming more popular, the nearest being Breakspear at Ruislip.

We arrived at the porch, the first photograph taken of my dad and I and my bridesmaids. I could hear the organ, and the perfume of flowers. I had chosen the music, with my fiancé's approval, and he the flowers. Oh, what flowers. Inside the door a triangle arrangement of cream roses, stephanotis maidenhair fern. As I walked down the aisle, 'Jesu, Joy of Man's Desiring' was played. The three front pews garlanded with more flowers, roses and ribbons in white and lilac. My fiancé turned to greet me with a smile and winked, held out his hand and kissed mine and said silently you look lovely. He too wore a navy double-breasted suit, immaculate cream shirt and a rosebud like my dad's.

We said our vows, clearly and word perfect, followed by the hymn 'Love Divine, All Loves Excelling', moved up to the altar and my fiancé gave me my platinum wedding ring with another vow. I had chosen 'Rustle of Spring' to be played whilst we signed the register. The vestry, a tiny room off to the side, Mummy and Daddy and my husband's parents had to wait by the door, as only my husband and I could stand together to complete the certificate details.

We moved down to the chancel steps. He picked a rose from the flower arrangement and gave it to my nan, together with a kiss from me. My nan had been in my life a great deal, especially when I was young. She always came and stayed during the summer when Mummy's asthma was really bad and she was confined to her room. I was the youngest grandchild and secretly knew her favourite. She was a real lady of spirit; widowed at thirty seven with four young children. My grandad, who I never knew, only by photograph, was in the navy and had died suddenly at thirty nine years. She decided she had to earn money for her young family and became a caretaker of Mutley Baptist Church, Plymouth. A small lodge house went with the position and that is where they lived until her children married. When she retired, she spent her years taking in turns with her children and their families. Each child had one child each. Two boys and two girls, ranging from eleven to me, the youngest. More than her other children, she spent more time with my mamma because of her frail health. She died in 1960, aged eighty six, and left a small house to each of her children and left money to me for a coach built pram for my baby that was due in early September that year. I was so glad she was aware about my baby news and promised, if a girl, would have her name, Ann. She was a very astute lady – wrote poetry, played the squeeze box, naturally amusing and although born in Victorian times, very broadminded and understood human nature.

We came out into the sunshine to Toccata in F by Widor. It was so hot, I was beginning to wilt and my lace dress felt prickly and overwhelming. I wished I had chosen a short-sleeved dress and lower neckline, breaking with tradition. More photographs, horseshoes given for luck and as we walked to our car, confetti and more confetti. My new husband helped me with my dress and veil, one last photograph getting in the car. We kissed at every opportunity – traffic lights, junctions, the windows open, so hot. We waved to everyone and hoped they felt as happy as we were.

We arrived at the Station Park Hotel. Our reception was in a large reception room upstairs. There were more flowers on window sills and on the long trestle tables in the shape of a T.

Fifty-four guests had been invited.

Sherry was served to the guests as we lined up to greet them.

My dad took us on one side and quietly said, "We have a three tier problem". The baker delivering our wedding cake, his helpers had put the cake on its tier stands, lifted it out of the van, lost balance and promptly dropped the whole cake in the street! We were both upset and my parents really annoyed, so for photographs we held the knife and cut pretending into the silver plinth.

My husband as usual made light of the situation and said, "I'll buy you another for our silver wedding or our diamond". The promise was kept for our silver.

We were announced by the toastmaster and walked hand-in-hand to the top table. We devoured prawn cocktail, roast chicken, new potatoes, runner beans (my favourite), carrots and gravy, followed by fruit salad and cream. On my request cheese and biscuits (I love cheese), coffee, all accompanied with icy Hock and liqueurs on request. My dad gave an amusing speech, tinged with his joy and love I had brought into his wife and his life. He thanked my husband for loving me and being the son he never had and how proud he was on this happy day.

The best man did the honours to the very attractive bridesmaids. My husband thanked my parents for me and this perfect day, and all the friends and family that attended.

My uncle (the engagement ring) also gave an extra speech, saying he told my parents after knowing my husband in the first week of 1951, "Ettie and Ted, this is the one for Valerie, you mark my words, and today we have the perfect match".

I'm glad in hindsight – glad not a good word, readers will know what I mean – that all three of them did not know what happened. They would be so sad and disillusioned that my dearest husband lost his way. He was such a shining young man.

We went around the room, speaking to our guests and thanking them for the gifts given. We were leaving around 5:00 p.m. Our best man offered his car. I asked my husband if we could walk back to my home to change – it was approximately six minutes away. I wanted to wear my dress a little longer. He was amused and agreed. We were walking arm-in-arm and people passing, curious and bemused.

One lady said, "Have you just got married?"

My reply: "Yes, I'm running off with the best man!"

I guess there was a very surprising conversation in her house that evening.

My husband helped me with the fifty buttons, hung my dress on the wardrobe. I dressed in a light wool navy suit, fitted jacket, straight skirt with trimming at the neck, and cuffs of white voile with navy dots. I never wore hats, but Mummy insisted and a navy blue straw boater with a daisy on the brim was put in place. It came off when I was out of sight. My accessories were navy and I wore very high-heeled navy court shoes.

My husband had also changed into a light grey suit.

We left our luggage in the hall and walked back to our reception. The best man's car was bedecked with ribbons, tin cans and a large Just Married on the bumper.

I suggested we had one more photograph of us and our guests taken by the hotel owner, more relaxing than by a professional.

We said farewell to my parents, more kisses and cuddles and good wishes. My in-laws, my nan and Auntie Dot. I told her it was lucky she was there, as the dates had been altered and nearly didn't happen. We waved until out of sight.

We were staying at the Cumberland Hotel, Marble Arch, where Webster & Girling had their theatre kiosk. The hotel had very generously given a double room overlooking the park. We had tea, did not unpack as tomorrow we were catching a coach to Combe Martin, North Devon.

We went to the theatre in the evening, previously booked. The play, a comedy, was 'Hippo Dancing', Robert Morley in the lead. We sat in the stalls holding hands. It was very funny. We went to the bar in the interval and decided to really splash out and have a taxi back to Marble Arch.

We returned to our room. I had packed an overnight bag; my nightie, his pyjamas, shaving gear and toiletries. We had an enormous bed, king size, I guess. We were both so tired we did not make love, just lay in each other's arms and fell asleep.

Woken up by the maid and breakfast, it was 7:00 a.m. Our coach left at 8:30 a.m. and would take all day for the journey.

We arrived at our hotel 'The Pack of Cards'. It had fifty two windows, four doors to enter by and the rooms had a theme of hearts, spades, clubs and diamonds, and a bar called 'The Joker's Bar'. Appropriately, ours was hearts. It overlooked a garden. A four poster bed and very old, big furniture. After unpacking, we went down to dinner. There were about twenty people in the hotel. We were placed at a table next to a family – mum, dad, two pretty little girls. They asked us why we had come on a Sunday, not Saturday like everyone did. We teased them by saying it was a secret. They asked every day and we never let on and teased them to see if they could guess. By the end of the fortnight, we eventually gave in. They were so pleased and surprised. They collected pennies from the guests and gave us a delightful gift – a see-through little box of blue plastic pegs with flowers painted on them. I never used them and kept them for years. Again, mislaid in one of our house moves, worse luck.

Our honeymoon was everything I expected it to be, although I had no comparison to make. My husband was sweet, tender and a passionate lover, never demanding, not that I would have minded as I only wanted to please him and enjoy. We both had L plates. We loved each other so much, it was satisfying and good just to be one, and always there beside me.

We returned on the 28th to a different and new experience – adjusting to living with my parents and always thinking about our future home and plans.

* * *

This is the first part of my writing. I plan to write two more parts.

As I close, my 56th sixth wedding anniversary is next Saturday – fifty six years to the day.

I feel very melancholy and sad, so I shall continue at a later time.

PART II
August, 1954 – May 1991

Still starry-eyed, trying to be realistic, we returned to our jobs on Monday 30th August. My new husband was at Head Office in Portman Square and I to the theatre agency in Baker Street.

We went separate ways, although quite close in offices. He travelled on the tube from Wembley Central. It took him fifteen minutes from my parents' home walking, travelled to Bond Street, walked into Oxford Street, crossed near Selfridges into Portman Square. He left home at 7:45 a.m. I caught the 9:40 a.m. train, steam, Aylesbury to Marylebone line, the terminal. I walked down about a hundred yards past the National Farmers' Union Head Office to the side entrance of the agency. The main entrance faced Baker Street station. It was in a small arcade that had a rather nice coffee shop, which also sold deli food, run by a lovely Jewish family who came from Germany in the early thirties and really loved Great Britain and how they were embraced and given sanctuary in our country. They would see me coming and there was always a Kit Kat on the counter. It cost 3p. They gave me a little bluebird ornament as a wedding gift to bring me good fortune and waved every time I was in view. On entering the office, there was a switchboard manned by a lady called Lynny. She was a real Cockney and was a laugh a minute. She used to regale us with tales of her mischief with Americans during the war and her visits to the Hammersmith Palais. The directors' office was also in this area and he too always came in that entrance. I had never been in his domain and admit a little afraid. He was an impressive-looking man; six feet four inches tall, balding, in his fifties. I think his wife was younger. He had married quite late, I was told. He was quite gruff and always tipped his deerstalker hat. He wore plus fours in heavy tweed and drove an open-top Bentley. He was noticeable. Lynny was always cheeky and you would see a slight smile, otherwise no one rarely approached him. He had a lady secretary who came in four days a week. She was also quite remote too and never came in the staff room or the Christmas dinner and dance.

I went down an unstable wrought iron staircase to my tiny kiosk adjoining the record shop. I'm sure the record shop had not had a stock-take or dusting for years. I never knew either if the lady that ran it rented the premises or if it belonged to the agency.

The lady that ran the shop was a real character. Her name was Miss P. Treschock. One day I saw an envelope on the counter and her Christian name was Perdita. It really suited her. No one but no one ever called her anything but Miss Treschock. I called her the soft brown lady and I'll relate why. She wore the same clothes day in, day out. I hope she had two sets, for cleanliness purposes, or maybe they were cleaned over the weekend. She wore long box-pleated brown skirts. Her tops were always hanging in folds and kind of loopy collar lapels, long sleeves with cuffs secured with covered rouleau buttons. She wore thick lisle hosiery and always the same shoes; pointed toed button over with Cuban heels. Her coat had one large button covered in the same material. Her clothes looked very crêpy, never stiff, and you saw no outline of her figure underneath. She was about five feet eight inches tall, a kind face, rather bird-like, pointed chin, hazel eyes, and her hair was in an untidy bun on the top of her head, with fronds hanging over her brow and in her neck. At some time I think she had home-dyed it with henna colouring. It had faded and underneath her natural colour which was pepper and salt. I don't think she had ever been to the dentist. Her teeth were not a good feature. Maybe she did not bother. She rarely smiled and I never heard her laugh. She was a very proper lady and I don't think she ever crossed the line. She lived with her mother in a basement flat in the back streets of Paddington, never talked about her father or family. What you don't know, you tend to make up. I used to imagine her fiancé had been killed in the war and she had never loved again or her dedication to her mother was because there had never been a father in the picture – a terrible stigma, even in the fifties. Or she had been very rich and lost their money in the Depression – who knows?

She, with her mother, went on an old packet boat to Estoril in Portugal every year for three weeks; the last in June and two in July. The record shop was closed. I always asked if she had a good time and always the same reply: "Very nice, dear girl, thank you for asking." I was always 'dear girl'. Although I constantly told her to call me by my Christian name, she would ignore me and always go back to dear girl or my maiden name. It did not change, even when I was married.

She reminded me of Miss Haversham in Great Expectations and I can bring her into my memory very easily.

I returned to introduce my little girl years later. The shop was closed. I asked what had happened and no one knew. It was as if she had never been. I never knew where she lived, otherwise I would have tried to find out what had happened.

Paramount in our minds was saving enough money to buy a house. I earned £3.15 shillings per week and my husband approximately £14 per week. He had an increase every year after an appraisal. I had received an increase of five shillings in the three years I had worked in Baker Street. I asked for an increase when I was getting married. We will think about it. The usual answer. You always opened your wage packet in anticipation!

Within a month, my better half had three part-time jobs. Three nights a week behind the bar at a public house called The Green Man. To save money on transport he cycled twelve miles and return from 7:00 p.m. to 10:30 p.m., delivered meat for two local butchers on a Saturday, starting at 7:00 a.m. to 10:00 a.m., and 10:30 a.m. to 1:00 p.m., and home for a snack lunch and cycled to Watford from my parents' home in Sudbury Town to work in a high class tailors. He liked that job. He always looked smart and loved silk ties and all that went with it.

My parents always said he was the sharpest young man on the block, walking down the road. His overall wages for these three jobs was £8. Now we calculated, was 4 eight pounds was £32 per month = £384 per annum.

We also saved most of my wages. Although my parents protested, we gave them rental and food expenses and lived on my husband's salary – our travelling to and from work, going out once a week, usually to the cinema, always in the 1/9ds. We never went to the coffee shop anymore and maybe now and again, Mamma and Dad would treat us to a drink at the Black Horse on a summer's evening, sitting outside watching the world go by. My only outlay on a personal level was nylons, something I always thanked the Americans for. Silk was madly expensive and young women never liked lisle, which would hang like pleats on your legs. Lots of girls coloured their legs with fake brown stuff and drew a line as if they were stocking seams. Thank goodness when tights came into our lives. I never had the patience to do the former.

Living with my parents, I did not find it as easy as my new husband. He was very tolerant. It was very difficult for any spontaneity – being madly in love, I wanted my beau to chase me upstairs and make love. You just could not do that with three other people in the house. My uncle (the engagement ring one) now lived permanently with us too. There were always three other opinions if I asked a question and so conversation, among other things, was in the bedroom, and often that could be difficult as they were in the next room.

He would console me constantly and say it would not last. When you are young, time drags, especially if you have a goal and yet now in the winter of my life, it is a real enemy.

As my husband worked through Saturdays, and I too worked until 1:00 p.m., Saturday afternoons I usually spent going to look around shops. Sometimes, if Mummy was well enough, we would go together and I always gravitated to furniture stores.

The Grange furniture store opposite Harrow-on-the-Hill station was my favourite. It gave the impression that furnishing was changing pace and the content of this store reflected change. In the thirties a couple would furnish their home in always the same way – mahogany and walnut were the woods of choice. A three piece suite – settee and two armchairs, always in the same design. Dining table, four chairs and two carvers, an enormous heavy sideboard, placed and never moved again, housing table linen, china and glass. I think most of the middle classes never could afford a dinner service and one for everyday use and that stayed throughout life. Sometimes a trolley would be around, always wood with embroidered tray cloths done by the lady of the house, starched, very pristine and rarely renewed, and a nest of tables was really special. I never saw any placemats or coasters. Tablecloths were very common over a chenille-type cloth with fringe, always russet or brown colour. The overall appearance of most homes was dullness and décor not to show marks and practical for everyday living. Central heating was non-existent or fitted carpets. A coal fire was the norm – everyone sitting as close as safety allowed, leaving brown marks on your legs because you were too close. Elders taking priority. Fires were usually lit early evening and if you were at home during the day, you would grin and bear it. On the other hand, mothers did not go out to work and busied themselves cleaning, washing. That in our house was all day Monday – everything washed by hand, a blue bag to keep articles white, starching collars and cuffs, hanging on an airer after putting through a mangle. Weather permitting, pegged on a line the length of the garden. We wore more clothes than we do today. Bras, liberty vests with rubber buttons, vests, underslips. Pants were in for young girls, but drawers were the order of the day, after the age of thirty! Sometimes there were disasters – shrinkages and rubbing holes in garments after vigorous friction on a washboard. My mum's and nan's friends were always sore and red after washday. The first electrical appliance my dad bought my mother was a Servis twin tub washing machine. It was appreciated more than a diamond ring.

   Back to The Grange, the major change was wood. A company based at High Wycombe called G Plan made furniture in teak.

   It was very different and easier to move around. Coffee tables, end tables, chairs, armless so you could arrange in different ways and angles. Wing chairs – much more elegant, no more protruding handles – usually integral doors and drawers. Divan beds, sometimes with drawers for storage, and more huge lumpy wardrobes that stuck out, giving bruises. Fitted new wardrobes along the walls, bedside tables for soft lighting and maybe a telephone placed instead of running downstairs and the ring-ring stops! More and more people had a telephone. My husband used to joke he knew was winning when he met me – my parents were one of the few who had a telephone and a car! I can still remember our number – W 7642. I had a file with all the furniture leaflets which we would pour over Saturday evenings when Mum and Dad were playing Solo or poker with friends in the next room. Already, I had been to John Lewis in Oxford Street and asked for swatches with my curtains in mind. I knew exactly the colour scheme. I loved green. I still find it very easy to live with, being nature's colour. I will enlarge later on décor, when we get our first home.

My next narration is about Christmas 1954 – our first celebration when my husband didn't have to go home each day.

I love Christmas. Mum and Dad were having twelve people to Christmas lunch. My nan, auntie and uncle recently returned from Gibraltar, four friends they played cards with and us.

Everyone contributed. Nan made the Christmas pud and cake, vegetables supplied by friends. My dad bought a bottle of gin/sherry/whiskey – wine was, I believe, not in the agenda in homes like ours. Generally, alcohol was in homes for medicinal purposes. My husband's parents were invited, but declined. We visited them every week and my parents asked them to supper, but they never gave a reason why they did not socialise. My father-in-law was always wrapped up in his health and his mother, I felt, just did not have the confidence. My father-in-law was very controlling and always putting Mum down and I'm sure if you live with someone like that, you come to believe you are useless. I remember her saying that although she loved him in her life, when he died it was relief, not grief, that brought the tears. Unfortunately, it was too late for her.

Christmas Day started as normal. Quite a great deal of activity in the kitchen, although forward planning was on numerous lists. Turkeys were collected on Christmas Eve, hanging bodies in every butcher's shop. We always had a large capon. My nan thought they were not so dry as turkeys. One does not hear of them anymore. Something to do, I believe, with European control. Everything on the table made by the hostess or friends, bread sauce, cranberry, no frozen vegetables, often pork accompanied poultry and always a ham cooked for Boxing Day. Always the dreaded Brussels sprouts. I would ban them even leaving Belgium – ha ha. Lunch was always on time – 1:30 p.m. The males usually had a drink either at the local or at home. Ladies sherry sipped in the kitchen whilst busying in laying the table or in the kitchen. That meant when we had our fill it was time for the Queen's speech at 3:00 p.m. I vividly remember, my dad always stood during this time and would toast with us all her health and you did not speak whilst she was speaking.

As soon as it was over, the dishes were put in soak. Hopefully, a lather was made up with soap and the games began. There were no detergents in those times.

Always, but always, charades, pass the parcel, musical chairs, or board games; Monopoly, Ludo etc., and cards. I remember my dad always did the forfeits and when it fell to him, he had to obtain some manure, he disappeared for over an hour. When he returned, bucket in hand, he had remembered a rag and bone man who had a horse, like Steptoe & Son. He had obliged and Dad stayed on for a couple of whiskeys too.

At seven o'clock a buffet-style meal commenced – rabbit pie, pasties, pickles and chutney, beetroot or sandwiches. The men drank beer and the ladies had port and lemon or a gin and orange. My tipple was Babycham in a Bambi glass and my dad always bought in a pack, just for me.

During the evening, the visitors and my parents played Solo or poker and we went into the other room. I played the piano and had a singsong or watched television or mainly played records on the Ferguson record player my parents bought me for my twenty-first birthday. We opened our gifts around 6:00 p.m. I still had a stocking in the morning. Presents were usually homemade and never expensive, like today. Handkerchiefs, handmade sewing cases (I've still got mine), socks, cigars. My dad nearly always gave my mum a brooch and one year bought pearl earrings. My husband knew how I had seen a table lamp in The Grange. Unbeknown to anyone, he had asked the store if he could measure and draw the article. He went to the library and got a book on making lampshades. He always said you could learn anything from a book.

He gave me his efforts as my present. Everyone was very impressed. It was great and did not cost £35. I commissioned another for my future side tables. He also had pressed a rose from my wedding bouquet in my friendship book and I still have it.

Most of us returned by 11:00 p.m. We had been delegated to sleep next door, which was not unusual, as my dad was always bringing folk home. Some looking for people and relatives that had lost touch or moved away after or during the war.

My husband said he thought we ran a B&B. My parents were very generous and would help anyone.

Boxing Day was again the same format. Neighbours were invited in for a drink, sausage rolls, mince pies, Christmas cake, pastries, trifle, blancmange, apple pie and my nan's homemade Devonshire cream – slowly boiling the top of the milk – cream – and then removing with a spatula and put in a bowl to cool, covered by a fine net with beads to weight it down. I still have the cover.

My nan was a very astute lady. Widowed at thirty eight with four children – three girls and a son. She was caretaker of a church on Mutley Plain, Plymouth. A little lodge house went with the position. All her children except my mother contributed and worked. Mum was never well with her asthma, put down to the damp and hilly terrain in Devon. When she married my dad she was still not well, but easier, in London. Strange, considering the fogs and pollution. She did have a really good doctor, who was more than interested in asthmatics and the causes.

Nan's eldest daughter, Elsie, at seventeen, went into service to a very wealthy building family and did an Upstairs/Downstairs and married the son of the house, who was twelve years older, called David. He died the same day I was born. The telegrams passed each other. She, like my nan, was a very young widow with two small children. A girl, eleven, and boy aged eight. He also died the same year as his father in 1933, of a mastoid complication. They were buried in the family plot in Plymouth. She never married again, inherited property and lived a very easy life. She died aged ninety eight.

Her daughter, my cousin, was privately educated and lived with her mother. They did everything as a team, until in her early forties she married. My aunt was not well pleased and lived with them all their married life. A great mistake. When she died they were in their seventies and my cousin's husband died only three years after my aunt, so they never had any time together without my aunt. They never had any children. My aunt always came first. Her son-in-law was a saint, as she was difficult in manner and very covetous, and distanced herself from the family.

My nan's son, Archie, was totally different – very funny and always in good humour. He was a stocky man, about five feet seven inches tall, wore spectacles and never seemed to take life too seriously. He trained in electrical engineering and worked for BT. His job moved him to Kingsbridge – a lovely part of Devon. Dartmouth was not far away. Kingsbridge was on an estuary and their houses were overlooking the water as they were tiered. It was very pretty. Holidaymakers flocked there and all along that coastline. It was only about thirty five minutes from Plymouth. My uncle used to travel around a great deal. I don't know what he actually did. Everyone knew him. He was very well-liked and I believe quite a practical joker.

In his late twenties, he met and married a lady called May Ellis. She was the only daughter of a master bakers family, the only one in Kingsbridge. From her photographs she was very pretty, slim, dark really curly hair and very fashionable. A real twenties flapper. My mother said she had violet eyes and all the boys wooed her. My Uncle Archie won. They had one son, Brian, my cousin. He was three years older than me. During the war I would visit them and we always had a fun time. My uncle and aunt had a lovely detached house up on a hill overlooking the town. It had lots of attic rooms and we played house and hide-and-seek and you could disappear all day in an acre of garden. They also had a vegetable and fruit garden. It was my first taste of gooseberries, raspberries and loganberries, with Devonshire cream, of course. I did not see much of Brian in my teens and twenties, as he married and moved away to Streatham. We always, when we did meet later in life, would reminisce about our happy times. He sadly died very suddenly in his early sixties, similar to his father. His mother, Auntie May, outlived him for many years. She moved away from Kingsbridge when widowed and lived in a bungalow near Torquay, again at the top of a hill. She died in her nineties.

The next child for my nan was my mother. Of my nan's four children, as I have said, Mummy always ailed. My nan was amazed she got to five years. Rarely attended school on a regular basis and was cosseted and spoilt by her family. As a child spent most days in bed or sitting on her father's lap, as he was asthmatic too. He died in his late forties from pneumonia complications and respiratory factors. Unlike now, little was known about asthma and no medication. Allergies were unknown. Not moving around seemed the only help and staying indoors. It was always worse in the spring and summer, known now to be the pollen count rising. It is when happening, an asthma attack, very distressing, both for the sufferer and onlooker. I knew my dad thought Mum's heart would fail whilst she was gasping for air. It was only later in life when she had adrenaline injections it was eased. Her arms were like pin cushions, bruised and sore. My dad would not let a draught blow on her, was a great carer and would support her always and never, ever complained. He told me that when he saw her for the first time at the Wembley Exhibition, he knew she was the one. Mummy was going to be engaged to a naval officer. Nevertheless, as I have related before, my mother was visiting her cousin. They lived in Wood Green, N.22. Dad met Mum on a Saturday and followed her home to Plymouth the following Friday. Asked my nan if he may marry her and my nan really liked him, which was always a bonus as they were married three weeks later on 18th April, 1926.

Daddy whisked her off to London. They had a first floor flat in Kensington and I was born there seven years later. He always called my mother his sweetheart and me his 'best girl'. She died aged seventy eight in 1981 and my dad in 1975, aged seventy five.

The last child of my nan's was my Auntie Dot. Her name was Dorothy Gwendoline. Again, a tiny baby, always called Dot by all the family. She was small-boned and dainty and very with it in appearance. Again, from photographs, smart and very attractive. She had a lovely singing voice and sang at dinners in big houses of the gentry. My mother told me that the Foot family, one of their sons, Dingle, tried to woo her. She was not interested and two years after my parents married, she married a very good-looking, fair-haired young man. He was a very quiet, refined young man and worked in the dockyard in Devonport. He was not a strong man and two of his brothers died of tuberculosis. I believe his mother also had tuberculosis. Rife in the twenties, sanitariums everywhere. If money was available, wealthy families went to Switzerland!

Auntie Dot and Uncle Ern had one child, like the rest of my nan's children, a son, Raymond. He was nine months older than me and of all my cousins, I spent more time in my formative years. He was like the brother I never had. Every year, from the age of six, my parents would put me on the Royal Blue coach at Hammersmith, taking all day travelling to Plymouth. My name and address was on a label attached to my coat and one piece of luggage. They would ask the driver to keep an eye on me at every stop en route. He would hold my hand and with other passengers, go into cafés for lunch or coffee breaks. When we stopped at Honiton for a cream tea, I knew I would see my cousin, auntie and uncle at the coach stop on Mutley Plain, nearly opposite the church where my parents were married.

I slept with my nan if she was also staying with her daughter. She gave me a peppermint sweet every night before I went to sleep, as a treat. She made it herself and I haven't tasted a better peppermint before or since. If she was staying with my mother in London, I had a big double bed to myself. My cousin slept in a smaller room at the front of the house. My auntie and uncle lived in the same house all their married lives and my cousin was born at home in April 1932. Home births were the norm. Maybe that's why the mortality rate was high, as if there were complications, there was only a midwife attending.

I know sometimes I was a hindrance to my cousin. Every day during the summer holidays he went out with his friends. They were like a Just William gang, even had a ginger, a boy called Bobby Rangford – a smiley boy covered in freckles. They used to let me come too, the only girl of course. They didn't think I'd join in their escapades, but I always did. My auntie's house overlooked Home Park, the home of Plymouth Argyle. It had a very steep bank with paths on one side and then paths went upward to a long ridge and then flattened out on the main park. They had a camp on one bank covered with foliage and we would take bottles of lemonade, sandwiches, sweets, apples etc. and play cowboys and Indians, fighting. I remember I was being a pain, so they tied me to a tree and left me – hours, and it was only a passer-by who set me free. They let me ride their bikes and generally were very tolerant. I was always being asked when I was going home.

I had a happy time and being the only girl, I was spoilt by my auntie and uncle. On one holiday my cousin caught chickenpox and I did too. We were both kept in bed and rigged up a string with a tin to our rooms. We would send notes and sweets to each other, moaning how we were missing playing. At weekends Auntie and Uncle would take us to the beach or countryside on the moors and places I liked was Clearbrook or Wembury, where we paddled in the river and caught newts and minnows. We walked everywhere and one weekday my cousin and I walked to Rowborough, eight miles. We were so tired, we went into the Rowborough Hotel and asked the staff to ring our parents to come and fetch us. We were both asleep in an armchair in reception when they turned up. My auntie and uncle were not pleased and we nearly got told off, especially as we had walked on a main road and so far. My cousin and I were great friends and in our twenties, when we both first married, shared the same house. I'll tell you about that later.

This narrative has been about my nan's four children. She died aged eighty six in 1960. I was always pleased she knew I was expecting her first great-grandchild and she left me many wise notions; a wonderful letter saying I was her favourite grandchild. I gave my daughter her name. I was given her name too, a second Christian name. She left a house to each of her children, that she had bought during her widowhood. She left me her lovely engagement ring. Sadly, it disappeared. My mother always had suspicions where it went. My nan died in her eldest daughter's home. She didn't die of any specific illness. She said she was tired and faded away. She is buried with her husband in Efford Cemetery in the family plot. I have visited it many times, but guess when I leave there will be no one left in my family who will remember. I am the youngest and have outlived all my cousins and family.

After Christmas 1954, we went into New Year 1955 with high hopes that we could have our own home by the end of the year.

My twenty-second birthday was, as always, celebrated with a party. Although we were the only married couple, we saw and were always included with our former friends. Most of them had girlfriends and boyfriends and one or two engaged.

During the Christmas break, I had thought for quite a while of leaving the agency in Baker Street. Prospects very low and no increase in salary. My season ticket had increased and I hardly saved anymore to swell our joint account. I talked it over at length with my husband and parents. They all agreed, but said the decision was mine. I did not want to give my notice in until I had found another position. I scanned the Wembley Observer every Friday.

Two weeks into the new year, an advert in clerical, advertised a P.A. job in an estate agents in North Harrow. I thought maybe I was setting my sights too high. Anyway, I wrote a letter, giving my qualifications in business studies, shorthand typing skills, including a S.A.E. which was the norm. Postage was 2½p, can you believe? I received a reply inviting me to an interview the following Saturday at 11:00 a.m. I was very nervous, as it was only the second interview I had experienced.

I wore the navy suit I wore on my honeymoon. My certificates from business college and a personal reference from a friend of my dad's, saying I was honest, trustworthy and loyal.

The agency was on a corner, with three windows onto the street advertising houses, flats and maisonettes and also letting accommodation, only yards from North Harrow station and opposite the Headstone Hotel.

A young lady, the receptionist, who I knew was younger than me, took me upstairs to the owner and director's office. The estate agents was called Warner & Co. I was ushered into Mr Warner's office; a large room with filing cabinets, leather-topped desk, tray of glasses and a water jug, plus a decanter and sherry glasses. Dark blue carpet on the floor and two carver-type chairs.

I sat down and within minutes Mr Warner entered. I'm not very good at ages, but I guess he was in his late forties, balding, smiley eyes in a kind face, about five feet eleven inches tall and nice hands. He had a navy pinstripe suit, double breasted. He looked very smart and slim. He shook hands, asked me where I had worked before, why I was leaving and then gave me a rundown on the office everyday routine. He also told me he had a smaller office at Rayners Lane, managed by a Mr Olive. If I was employed for six months I would have the responsibility of that office – typing survey reports, details of properties and a register of prospective buyers. The hours would be 9:00 a.m. to 12:30 p.m., 12:30 p.m. to 1:30 p.m. lunch break, and finish at 5:00 p.m., working every other Saturday 9:00 a.m. to 12:30 p.m. The salary was twice what I was getting at Baker Street, two weeks' holiday and another week at Christmas. As people did not go house hunting a solicitors also did not work until the new year. I would also have extra duties accompanying Mr Warner to lunches, to take notes re. mortgages etc. These would be with building society management.

I learnt afterwards, a great deal of business was done on the golf course in those days. Mortgages were granted by quota per month. Later on, our home was agreed that way.

Mr Warner had interviewed two other applicants, but on the spot he said he would be delighted to offer me the position. He also added that when his secretary left, she was moving away from the area, I would replace her and come into the North Harrow office, approximately in six months' time.

I thanked him profusely and hop, skipped and jumped to the station and came home. Mummy was having a rest, my husband playing rugby, my dad mucking about in the garage. I was bursting with my good news. Needless to say he was pleased for me and that evening we would have a celebratory drink.

It goes without saying everyone was pleased and assured me that I had made the right decision.

I told Mr Warner I would have to give a week's notice on the following Friday. I decided to have a week's break and start my new position in fourteen days. Now, I had to buck up courage to say farewell to the theatre agency. It is always difficult to say goodbye to friends and a job I had always really enjoyed, plus the marvellous spectrum of theatre and entertainment I had enjoyed over the years.

I must add that Mr Warner told me if I was not happy or had any problems, I must not hesitate to tell him. He reminded me very much of my dad, both in looks and manner.

On Monday morning, I knocked on the door of the general office manager, Mr W. Wallis. May I tell you something? Before I could enlarge, he smiled and said was I expecting? I said no, I would like to give my notice. I explained the reason, mainly salary, plus when I had my own home I would not want to commute up to London every day. He was understanding and offered to ask for a rise in wages, but I assured him I knew it would not be forthcoming, plus I was still only a 'go for' with little stimulation for shorthand etc. He said all the right things and how sorry and I would have a shining reference. He said of course there would be a 'whip around' and would I like a gift or the money? I asked for the money.

Every day one or other of the staff said they would not replace me as I was the best 'go for' ever and wouldn't I change my mind. Several employees agreed the salaries were mean and many had the same wage as when they started. Married men with families. It just couldn't happen now. Very short-sighted, as loyalty should be rewarded. People rarely left their jobs in those days. I think they conformed and were afraid of change, understandably after the war years.

Friday came, my leaving. I did feel miserable and knew I would feel sad saying au revoir. I arrived at the office, usual time. I didn't settle to anything, tidied my little kiosk. Waiting for me a lovely posy of flowers from the coffee shop, plus a lovely chocolate éclair, my favourite, and a card with good wishes for the future.

I listened to some records being played in the record shop, had a cup of coffee. At around 12:00 p.m. a colleague asked me to go into the staff room, also in the basement. One person was left on the front counter, otherwise all the staff were there.

I was given more flowers, a sealed envelope, lots of hugs and good wishes. I thanked everyone, but was overwhelmed and went back to my little office. Mr Gamble, the senior clerk, came in and said you can go home, as time will drag for you just sitting around, and I decided just that, as it was not a usual day.

I walked up to Marylebone Station after saying goodbye to my friends in the coffee shop and promised I would come and see them whenever in the area. The train was empty, except for some shoppers. I had a compartment to myself, opened my envelope and five crisp white tissue notes of £20 amounting to £100 was enclosed. So generous and such a boost to our funds. I wrote to each and every one of the staff. I can still remember their names and I list below, which will conclude this happy time in my first job:

Mr F. Gamble (senior clerk), Mr Frewin (front desk), Mr W. Wallis (general manager), Mr S. Hebron, Lynny on switchboard, Miss S. Benfield, Eve (postal duties), Mr K. Webster (director), Mr A. Buckingham, and of course Miss Treschock.

I settled into a new routine easily, leaving home at 8:45 a.m. I had a key to open the office. Sometimes Mr Olive would be meeting clients viewing properties and would appear later. I was essentially to do details of properties, run them off on a photocopier and send to clients on a register every fourteen days, answer the telephone and clients' requirements etc. I liked the passing public coming in and chatting re. finance, mortgages and where they wanted to buy a house. Mr Olive was very pleasant and easy to work for. I was aware he was a ladies' man as some clients, always attractive ladies, were taken into his office and the door shut! It didn't bother me, as he was very proper to me.

Head office had three other single girls in the office, an insurance broker, three estate agents and Mr Warner, the owner of the company, so again I was the only married young woman.

Mr Warner knew my house plans and said when we were ready to let him know and he would look to finding a property in and around Harrow/Pinner. I was not so stressed, as I felt our goal was getting nearer every day.

There were no weddings that year, of friends. My cousin who had moved to London, working in the Civil Service and lodging near my parents' home, was getting engaged to his sweetheart Jo, who had been in his life since sixteen. They met at Grammar School and then later the same church. Jo worked in the Post Office and travelled around the West Country. They had a long distance courtship, but rock solid commitment. They planned to marry in 1956. Jo came from a very loving family and sadly lost a brother from meningitis, aged five. Her father was a Commander in the navy.

In early October 1955, my dad was fifty five and he invited us with Mummy to have a meal at 'Snows' in the Strand. Going 'up West', as he said, was always a treat.

We met my husband. Dad had booked a table and I think it was the first time we had wine with our meal.

During the evening, Dad asked us how our bank balance was going. We had saved £740. He said, as promised, I'll double it – go look for a house.

In those days, a 10% mortgage was needed, plus solicitor's fees, and we set our sights at a semi-detached house and garage, approximately £2,000, with a £200 deposit, plus we could afford furniture and maybe a washing machine/oven. My nan had offered, in fact insisted, to buy carpets and with our wedding presents we would be fine. We were going to make it in under two years. I was and know my better half was excited.

I, of course, told Mr Warner about this event and he promised he would make it a priority to find us a house.

Christmas was around again. We had a great office party across the road at the Headstone. I was fortunate to have pleasant colleagues to work with once again. Of course, having a complete week off, returning on my birthday, which ignited another celebration – drinks at lunchtime. Mr

Warner's wife had made a lovely cake and more gifts for 'that house!'

In February, Mr Warner said he had viewed a house on what was known as the County Estate. All the roads were named after a county. It was a corner property on Sussex Road, built by a builder called 'Cutler' in the late thirties. Bay windows, upstairs and down, front door with overhanging porch, detached garage, three bedrooms, galley-type kitchen, French doors in the downstairs back room, long garden to the rear with an apple tree and side beds. Because it was a corner property, the aspect faced down the road, up the road opposite and again a road to the other side, so the traffic had to slow down which was an advantage. At the top of the road, about seventy five yards, was the main road to Harrow-on-the-Hill in one direction and to North Harrow and Pinner in the other direction, approximately five minutes from Warner's. The price was lower than usual for this type of house. It was leasehold – there would be the opportunity to buy the lease at a later time. We viewed and liked it very much. It was the first step on the property ladder. Our offer was accepted. Our mortgage went through without a hitch and exchange and completion was dated for the beginning of April. The property was empty and Mr Warner asked the vendors if we could have access to do decorating etc. My husband set to, as always, painting, although wallpaper was the 'in' fashion. We both agreed on plain walls, lining paper with matt finish emulsion. The hall had a border of wood, half way up the wall. We kept it the same, just changed the colour. We have so many low grey ceiling days in this country, I liked light décor then, and still do, whatever the fashion décor. Our sitting/dining area was in a pale fresh green, white paintwork. Our bedroom a hint of pink. We had been given as a wedding gift a raspberry colour eiderdown and bedspread. The kitchen had no tiling, a butler sink, a coal boiler for heating water. No central heating as it was still in its infancy and very expensive to install.

The exterior was fine and we painted our front door, wine red.

As I mentioned before, my cousin was getting married in June 1956. I can't remember where the idea came from – my cousin, like us, could not find anywhere to rent and like us also would eventually want their own home. By mutual agreement, plus it would help us financially, we would convert the upstairs. The third bedroom would be their kitchen, the upper front room, their sitting/dining room, and the other double room overlooking the garden, their bedroom. We would share the bathroom. We converted the large cupboard under the stairs to a toilet, so really we had a rota re. bathing as we all had different time schedules to leave for work that did not cause any problems. I left the house last, as my office was only five minutes away. My cousin was in London and mine was now at a new depot in Southall and my cousin's wife Jo worked.

So once again, my cousin I had spent so many happy times when we were young, were sharing married life with our partners.

My husband went to a crash course on plumbing and general DIY, did the upstairs conversion kitchen, and when we moved in it was grand. We bought our G Plan furniture, went to the Ideal Home Exhibition and bought a Belling cooker and Servis washing twin tub. I have always loved china and glass and I had been buying one plate at a time of 'Spode' in plain white with an embossed border, which I still have later. When we could afford it, we bought Royal Worcester which would be mixed and matched for special occasions. We moved in 4th April, 1956, so we had the house to ourselves, before my cousin and his new wife moved in after their honeymoon in Jersey at the end of June. They were married in St Gabriel's Church, Peverell, Plymouth, where they had worshipped since their teens. We attended with my parents.

We always visited our in-laws once a week. They never showed any interest in our house activities and I cannot recall them ever visiting. I always felt sad for my husband, their apathy, as he was a good son and later when our finances improved with his promotions, he bought them fitted carpets, had central heating installed and numerous other luxuries for them, that they would never have had. Never a sincere thank you or gesture of appreciation.

His brother had joined the Merchant Navy for two years to avoid National Service and on leaving, had to do National Service as well. He never showed any stability or direction in his career. His parents, it was very clear, thought he could do nothing wrong and when he was younger, he would sell articles that belonged to my husband, and although it was not done in a sneaky way, his parents never reprimanded him, passing it off as boys will be boys. I'm sure if it had been the other way round my husband would have been called to order. He got up to all kinds of mischief and his brother always bailed him out, as he knew his parents would be very upset. Whenever I took a stance about these happenings, my husband would defend, saying he could have been institutionalised. They did look after him, just never showed any affection or praised him for his achievements. Parents so different from mine. I did not really understand it.

There are no books on parenting, no doubt because we are all different, but love is very easy to give. It's all the prejudices that get in the way and they only seem to surface in adulthood and there seems no answer. It happens in every generation.

Everything was tickety-boo. We enjoyed so much our first home. We got on very well with our upstairs. My cousin and my husband both had the same Christian name and my mother's maiden name was also the same, so my nan's surname was also the same. It could be quite confusing at times. I always called my partner by his full length Christian name and my cousin the shortened form to make the difference. We had one of the country's most common of names, the second most popular name in Wales.

Like my parents, our home was full of friends and one couple especially, they lived in Essex. He was a colleague in the same company as my husband. He was always called Johnny and his wife was another Jo, short for Josephine. She also worked in head office. They had been married over ten years and were older than us. They lived in a flat over Jo's mother's wool shop in Billericay and their pride and joy was a boat moored at Little Holland. They spent most weekends on the boat. I didn't think Jo was so enamoured – it was Johnny's toy. They were a great fun couple. No moods or tempers and we enjoyed being with them. Johnny loved his food and took us to so many different cuisines. It was, I feel, lost on me, but my husband really enjoyed. Johnny knew loads of people and you only had to say about an idea and he would put it into practice. They were very generous and we became very fond of them. Later, we chose them as godparents to our baby. It was very sad for us when years later their marriage failed. Jo wanted a family, Johnny did not, as his boat was a substitute. Jo had a baby daughter and it all went wrong, as John did not like the competition and that's what eventually split them up. He left Jo for someone else. She was devastated, as were their parents. Johnny went his own way, never saw his little girl and died in his fifties with a heart attack. Jo and I kept in touch for many years, but again our meetings and letters dwindled and we lost touch. I have always been disappointed that what started as a deep friendship is no more, and also for our daughter being her godparents. I think of them very often.

In 1957, my bridesmaid Dorothy got married, yet again to someone in my husband's company. He was in head office all of his career and never on the road. He was called John. They were married in March and I was their matron of honour. Then in July, two more close friends got married at the same church as us. Jean and David. David lived in the same road as my parents' home, across the road in fact. David always came to my parties and we went out together in our teens to the Albert Hall and dances until my better half came on the scene. David was a great cricket enthusiast and played for a local team, and steam trains as well was a great interest. I remember his wife Jean went to the County Grammar School and was in a form below my husband, so we had good ties. When they married they lived in Petts Wood, Kent. They commuted to the City every day. Jean worked at the Bank of England and David on the Baltic Exchange. Later, in 1960, we both had babies, but I'll enlarge on that in another chapter.

In 1958, two memories come to mind.

Later in that year, my husband was taking over a new depot in Chalfont St Giles. He was going to be promoted to an area manager from a branch manager. His salary had increased and our bank balance, healthy. In May we bought a Lambretta. It was pale blue, second-hand and in good condition. I was apprehensive, as one feels very vulnerable out there among lorries, cars etc., although traffic wasn't so dense as it is now. It was the only time in my life I wore trousers. You really needed them in the cold and it was safer. Skirts flapping near an engine can be very dangerous. It was not compulsory to wear helmets. Of course, my dad insisted for all the right reasons. It did give us great independence. My Uncle Archie and Auntie May (Mummy's brother) invited us to their home for a summer holiday. We decided to do the journey on our Lambretta. We obtained a map from the AA for the journey. We could take little luggage, so only one case was acceptable which would sit behind me. Although my parents did not say anything, I knew they were apprehensive. We were staying for a fortnight and left on a Saturday morning. We had sandwiches and a flask of coffee. We planned on stopping every hour, as concentration was very important. We thought it would take all day, hoping to arrive early evening. We had good weather which was good and soon were travelling on the A30 to the West Country. Conversation was limited, because of noise, so only instructions and the occasional are you okay? comes to mind. Because the scenery was new, travelling this way, time went quickly. The biggest challenge was just past Exeter. A new road had recently opened – three lanes with very high sides of rock. I think it was called Telegraph Hill. To me it looked like a mountain. Our small little engine was really labouring and started to overheat and came to a stop in heavy traffic, half way up the hill. Many people came alongside, but did not stop, the traffic kept moving. They commiserated and gave advice – wait an hour for the engine to cool and so forth. Anyway, we sat down on the side and did just that, waited over an hour. We were only grateful it was fine weather. We eventually arrived at approximately 7:00 p.m. We had to walk the machine up the hill to Uncle's house. In fact, it was so steep we did that every time during our stay.

Auntie and Uncle had a delicious meal waiting for us and after relaxing, Uncle took my husband down to the Kingsbridge Arms to meet his pals.

We had a great holiday – visited Dartmouth, Hope Cove, Loddiswell. Went up the River Dart and saw where my favourite tipple was made – Babycham – from the orchards on the riverbank. We also took a trip over to Kingsowen and many little bays with golden sand. Sunbathed, swam and took in the lovely Devon scenery. We went into Plymouth to see the Grand Parade, built after the war, as it was flattened during the bombing. Went on the Hoe and looked across the Sound. I remember my mother telling me she swam across to the breakwater. She was an excellent swimmer, in spite of her health problems. She looked very 'with it' in her twenties swimsuit. Not very flattering, I did not think, yet I'm sure it brought about admiring glances, as girls did not wear swimsuits often. I cannot remember the month we went on this holiday.

When we returned my cousin and his wife Jo had decided to buy their own house, which they duly did. A house very similar to ours, about a mile and a half away in North Harrow. Bought through Warner's, of course.

We were quite financially stable, so converted the third bedroom, which was their kitchen, back into its original use. It was great to have the whole house to ourselves, although it had been a happy time sharing. We now had a dining and sitting room, which overlooked the garden. Our bedroom was now upstairs in the front of the house. We could have visitors to stay and in two years' time, the third bedroom was filled with the most important little person in our lives. Writing about that event is yet to come, readers.

In 1959, as I have said before, we enjoyed having the house to ourselves. At least one weekend in a month we had Jo and Johnny to stay. My husband was very good in the kitchen. He genuinely enjoyed trying different types of food. I was always impressed, how he excelled at everything he was interested in. He did not pursue his sporting activities anymore, played tennis sometimes, usually liked spending time in our house and garden. He went to boxing with my dad and on one occasion saw Cassius Clay, who of course changed his name to Muhammad Ali. As agreed by everyone, the 'best'.

In June 1959, he was given another promotion and a company car – a Ford Escort. I was so pleased for him. In the five years since we married, he had gone from strength to strength. He was well-liked in the workplace and our love for each other had not diminished. Although he would not see me for a day, when he came home he kissed me as if it had been a week. He told me he loved me every day, still brought me gifts and flowers, called me the sunshine in his life.

He showed impeccable manners to me and my family and my dad said he was the son he never had. My dad never understood his parents' attitude and put it down to ignorance and bias. When my dad died in 1975, my husband wept openly.

My special friend I had in my convent days got married in 1957 to David. I did not warm to him. He was very controlling and bossy. He was commissioned during his National Service and could not get out of the habit of ordering people about, especially my friend. She was a sweet-natured young woman and never retaliated to his demands. Everything was planned, diagrams drawn, no spontaneity at all.

Anyway, they asked us to go on holiday with them. I hesitated, but my husband said you are not married to him, don't worry about it. On the other hand, I just did not like my friend being demeaned and constantly being told she was silly. I told him on several occasions about his attitude. He was so thick-skinned. He would look at me in disbelief that a member of the opposite sex should question his abilities. Nevertheless, we decided to go. My husband, I realise, had the right approach. He would laugh at him and David knew he could not impress with his bumptious ways.

MORE OR LESS

For the first time since our honeymoon, we stayed in a hotel – The Headland overlooking Perranporth Beach, near to Newquay, Cornwall. The view was spectacular and we lay in an enormous double bed listening to the sea. It was recorded as one of the hottest summers. The sand burnt your feet, if you did not wear sandals.

David had insisted on borrowing his father's big car, a Rover 2000, only to show off. I overheard him tell one of the guests it was his! He worked for the G.E.C. Electrics. I think every building we passed he had lit it! He was very good-looking and I can only think my friend took to his physical attributes and not his character, as we knew them a long time and he was always the same and never mellowed.

On that holiday most people we met had the measure of him. Every day in the first week he would appear on the beach in snorkel gear – flippers, a wet suit and spear. Of course the sea was not suitable for snorkelling, much too rough with rollers and breakers, suitable for surfers. His appearance always made for a lot of teasing and ribbing. One afternoon they went into nearby Newquay and the lads got up the fire escape to their room, which was next to ours. They harpooned his trilby hat, trousers and jacket to the wall. When he came down to dinner that evening he asked everyone re. this happening. Of course, everyone was innocent. The message did get through – he did not don his kit again, with the excuse the sea was not suitable. What a surprise!

My friend and I had so much in common. Our Christian names were the same, our birthdays even the same date. Later, we had our baby girls within days of each other. I was very fond of her and we were inseparable at school. I often wished she had found someone who respected and loved her for herself. She was much too loyal and moral to overstep the line. She confided in me, many years later, she knew her partner had sapped her confidence and self-worth. She had no one in her corner to rise above it. After my husband left, she was a dear, sending notes and cards to cheer me. On one occasion her husband telephoned, giving his views of course, always destructive and adding he did not want his family involved in the plot, whatever that meant. I wrote to my friend saying I valued our friendship and to keep in touch. I never had a reply. I have often wondered if he intercepted the letter. I sent a birthday card the following year, with another note. I never heard from her again. She did not have the strength to overcome her partner's influence, sadly. I still have her birthday in my birthday book and remember.

In my life I have been very fortunate, having many friends who were constant and true. Only one other friendship floundered.

I had met this friend when I was at Baker Street. She was five years older, extrovert. Her family lived not far from mine. She was on the front desk. We often went to the freebie theatre together. During my courtship, she had a failed engagement and decided to go into hotel management and became a receptionist in a hotel in Norfolk. We always kept in touch and when she met and fell in love with a lovely chap, an American, I was so pleased for her. Once again, I was her matron of honour on my twenty-seventh birthday in 1960. They had two daughters – one two months after us, followed by another baby girl two years later. It was a terrible shock when her husband suddenly died of a massive heart attack, aged forty five.

During this time, my husband was so supportive, helping in every way. This happened when they lived nearer to us. They had returned from America. My friend did not settle, found the pace of life not to her liking. Her husband was very Anglicised and they moved back to the UK and then this devastating shock. It was awful.

We were visiting and a disagreement started over something very trivial. I cannot even remember. The outpouring of resentment of being left and trying to cope etc. I knew how much she was hurting and said let's have some space and that I valued our friendship and things would be calm again and it was foolish to put our friendship in jeopardy over a triviality.

We returned home. I did not hear for another ten days and eventually sat down and wrote a note, saying please telephone and sent flowers, hoping this was the olive branch. Once again, I never heard from her again. Several years later, she wrote to me after hearing through the grapevine my husband had left, enquiring after my welfare and asking me to get in touch. I was pleased. After talking on the telephone she invited me to stay. I travelled by coach to Norwich where she met me. Within hours I knew I had been asked, not through friendship, but, I felt, to gloat over my situation. Again, only criticism, judgement, showing no compassion or understanding, like herself, years before had received. After a few days I came home, very sad and disillusioned. To add insult to injury, she sent back several gifts I had given her, requesting the postage and saying she did not want anything to remind her of me or my family.

I did adhere to her request, with a note that I was aghast at her manners and behaviour and again, I never heard from her again.

I have a friendship book and I bring to mind two quotations:

A friendship that can come to an end never really began

and

A friend will joyfully sing with you when you are on the mountain top and silently walk beside you through the valley of darkness.

I think of them very often with pleasure, always tinged with great sadness and regret.

Back to our holiday. We often would go down the fire escape and go skinny dipping after midnight, make love and talk of the future. We decided to have a baby. We had been married five years, had attained our goal – a house, a happy lifestyle – our future looked rosy. We both loved children and it seemed the natural next event.

My dad had hinted several times about the patter of tiny feet and I would tease and say when we have a refrigerator.

On our return from holiday, we bought a six foot Prestcold fridge/freezer. It was a monster in our kitchen. As soon as my dad saw it, I could see the baby signs in his eyes and sure enough, in four months I knew I was going to be a mother. He thought we were so clever.

In 1960 I had two love affairs that have lasted all my life. I will tell you in the right order.

In April, due to my condition, I was advised by my doctor to give up work. The usual experience of morning sickness lasting three months, lasted all day, every day throughout the following months. I was four months into my pregnancy. At least it would cease in five months!

I was bored silly at home, found it hard to concentrate. I spent a lot of time at my parents' home. It made the time go quicker, and always made an effort to make dinners for my husband. I never fancied anything, except cheese on toast. One Thursday afternoon, I was reading the Harrow Observer and there was under Pets for Sale, poodles – black miniatures, in nearby Harrow Wealdstone.

As I think I have said before, I had always wanted a dog. My dad was also a great dog lover and he would have bought me a dog, always in mind the hair problem and my mother's asthma, and said perhaps when you have your own home.

I walked over to the library and read as much as I could find about poodles. As is well-known, they do not moult and have no odour when wet, are clever, appealing, and like children.

I telephoned the number and a lady listened to my request and said you can come around now, we will have tea and discuss.

I caught the bus – it was three miles away – walked for about a mile, finding the house. It was a large, double-fronted and I expected to hear lots of barking. The door was opened by a very pleasant lady, about forty, name of Mrs Watson. I noticed immediately poodle pictures, rosettes, certificates. Still no noise. I was ushered into a nice room with sofas. No evidence of dogs. They asked me many questions: why I wanted a poodle, my circumstances. It still wasn't evident that I was a lady in waiting. I told them of my yearning always for a dog and explained re. my mother's health.

They nodded in agreement. Mrs Watson left the room to make tea and Mr Watson told me their kennel name was 'Petitbrun Poodles' and they bred black and chocolate dogs. They always did well at Crufts Dog Show and in the fifties had a winner.

Mrs Watson returned and told me some advice. When we let the puppies in, let the dog choose you, not the other way around. Dogs know when people like them. I said I understood, but I didn't really. Later, after having more dogs, I did. They disappeared into another part of the house and on opening the door, five bundles of curly-haired, black puppies bounced into the room. They were adorable. Full of energy, nibbling, licking, falling over each other. Just as Mrs Watson said, one little fellow jumped on my lap, cuddled up, licking my chin. He was inky black with amber eyes and a small rubber nose. I fell in love immediately. They smiled and said that's the one for you. I had not asked re. cost and when I recovered, they said he would be £50. I felt he was worth every note.

Mrs Watson gave me his pedigree paperwork. His mother was Beauty Blackcurrant and his sire, Big Apple Petitbrun. I learnt afterwards they called all their dogs after fruit. I thought this was unusual and funny. She also advised me on feeding and he needed another injection and then he could go on the pavement.

I returned home with my furry bundle, waited for my husband to come home. It did not occur to me he may disapprove. I was proved right. From that time, I had a poodle in my life and still have.

I suggested we drove over to see Mum and Dad that evening. My dad evidently said when he heard us arrive, I don't know what was under my arm – it looks like a black muff.

My dad fell in love too and could not leave him alone. My mother thought I was nuts, having a baby and a puppy. Her concerns were he would be jealous and bring problems. I had great confidence in nature and knew my little dog would shine through.

I had not thought of any names, determined not Chummy, Bubbles or Rover.

After a few days, I decided on Bumble B. He was always so busy and I had seen a cartoon strip in an evening paper about a fun dog called Bumble B. Also I thought it sounded 'Dickensian', like in Oliver Twist. It got shortened to Bumble. It really suited him. He responded to my voice and became very obedient, no doubt because I was with him all the time. He gave me exercise and instead of sitting around feeling nauseous, it made the days fly by.

Whenever I attended the hospital for check-ups, I did not put on weight, as is usual, and the obstetrician said my baby was always the wrong way round – the head was under my arm and legs across to the other side. He assured me babies near to birth nearly always get it right. He reckoned my pelvis was too narrow for my baby to be comfortable. On two occasions, they tried to move it into the right position. I would get on the bus and by the time I got home, it was back in its comfort zone. I was sure it was a boy – it played football all day in my tummy. I always had chronic indigestion and drank soda water for England.

It was a very hot summer. Some days I felt like a beached whale and terribly uncomfortable. I could not wait for September to come. My dad bought me a badge, saying 'Under Construction'. It raised a few high brows. I thought it was funny.

On leaving Warner's office, they were all so generous, buying nappies, baby blankets, a lovely white pram cover and pillow. My bridesmaid Pamela was a gifted knitter and made six matinee jackets, booties and mittens. My parents were buying a cot and out of their loft came a Moses basket which was recovered in Broderie Anglais. My nan, who had died in late January, left me some money to buy a coach built pram and one was on order from Selfridges – white with grey hood and accessories, and an umbrella sunshade. It was a Royal Pram.

My husband confided in me, he would like a baby girl, to start. I did not mind, as mothers do, as long it had ten fingers and toes and was healthy. A pigeon pair would have been fine. Of course in those days there were no scans or ultrasound, so there was excitement wondering. Something mums miss out now, but gain in other ways.

We had not set our mind on any boys' names. Definitely on a girl's – as remembered, the day I saw that lovely little girl's photograph in the director's office in Baker Street. As the name was always my idea, my husband would choose her second, and the family name of Ann, after my nan and myself. We had a very common surname and I hoped her Christian name would be foremost and impress.

The date came nearer and nearer. On a Sunday afternoon, we made our usual visit to my in-laws. I was not feeling very well and suffering from the heat. We left about 9:30 p.m. My father-in-law, as always, talking about himself. He only seemed happy to be miserable. There was no baby conversation with Mum and as always, salmon and cucumber sandwiches, Madeira cake or cherry, lashings of tea.

Our journey took approximately half an hour, driving slowly. The car went in the garage, I went indoors. I was running the bath to relax. I went to the toilet and I knew something was different.

I went downstairs and told my husband. He went into overdrive, ran out to take the car out, telling me to get my packed bag. I was rather bemused. First, babies could take ages to make an appearance and I wasn't going to the hospital yet. I went and sat down. He was frantic, rang the hospital and after a brief conversation, literally propelled me into the car. Good job it was late. He went through sets of red lights. I was protesting all the time. He tried to placate me by just saying you must go to hospital, you will be safe there. I felt perfectly safe where I was and even suggested we went to my parents. They would reassure him. It was to no avail and we arrived at the hospital around 10.45pm.

What struck me, was it was very quiet and dark. A dim light on in reception, with a nurse wearing plimsolls. My husband did all the talking as if I wasn't there, gave me a long loving kiss and went.

I waddled after him and said, "Where are you going?"

"To your parents, of course. I'm terrified."

I laughed. "You are terrified, that's rich! I'm having the baby."

He was through the doors and gone.

The little nurse smiled and said, "That's men for you, let's get you sorted".

In those days, there were no antenatal classes or anyone to tell you what to expect.

I was ushered into a cubicle, given a hospital gown, a narrow sofa-like bed with starched white covers and a light cotton blanket. The only other thing I noticed was a jug of water, no glass.

I undressed and put my things in a locker. The nurse came in again and proceeded to give me an enema – not the most pleasant of happenings. I was then led to a toilet and told not to close the door. Nothing was happening. No contractions. I felt sure it was a false alarm. The nurse brought in a gas and air machine and kept saying you will be fine and that a doctor would come soon. I lay down and snoozed off, what to me seemed a long time. A doctor gently woke me and asked how was I feeling. I assured him, there was a mistake, nothing was happening. He smiled and examined me and said we will keep you here and see if anything starts. In the early hours of the morning, the time seems double time. I was getting a dull ache in my lower back, but nothing spectacular. The little nurse came in at regular intervals saying well done and other phrases. I settled down, thinking this giving birth is tedious, but not half so painful as portrayed in the cinema and what other people had related to me. I even wondered if I could have breakfast as I fancied bacon and eggs. The nurse came in and told me I would go into the second stage soon, whatever that was. By 7:30 a.m. the place was buzzing, nurses everywhere, putting their heads around the door, giving me smiles and reassurance re. my progress. There was a girl in the cubicle down the hall making awful noises and I wondered if it was my turn next. It just did not happen. I was sure someone would come and tell me I could go home. My due date was almost four weeks away and besides, it was a Monday and I realised August bank holiday. I thought if I have my baby today, like me she won't have any cards because it was a bank holiday and there was never deliveries of mail.

At approximately 8:45 a.m. three doctors and a nurse appeared. I was sure I was being sent home. One of them was Mr Fisk, the obstetrician I had seen many times and whose care I was in. The two other doctors were juniors, observing. Mr Fisk was a gentle man, with lovely blue eyes and cool hands, always an advantage for a doctor. He had always examined me covering with a sheet, so as not to embarrass.

He spoke quietly to them about some medical terms and then patted my arm and said, "Well, my dear, let's get this baby born. You will be prepared for the theatre and when you wake up, you will have your baby and all will be well".

I was overwhelmed with concern. I asked him why and he just said, "You can't do it yourself and your baby is getting distressed and wants to have a birthday".

Everything started happening very quickly. I remember going through the operating theatre doors and then nothing.

I woke up, still there, and Mr Fisk bent down and whispered, "You have a lovely baby girl".

I started to cry with relief. I asked could I see her. She was in an incubator as she had had a rough journey, but I was assured it was only temporary and would be in a crib by my bed in hours. She was considered a premature baby and not birth weight. I was taken after lots of stitches which felt uncomfortable, but you forget all the discomfort and only your little miracle.

I was in an end bed overlooking the garden. The ward was full of new mothers and they all waved and said who's a clever girl, asked me about my baby's gender and how I felt and had I thought of names.

It was a Monday, so my little girl would be fair of face. I too was born on a Monday, my husband on a Sunday.

The next episode I am going to tell you about rather stole my thunder and although not too important, was disappointing. Before I relate, I felt I had got off lightly in childbirth. I heard about experiences from my bedfellows and one girl, she was Irish, vowed she would not have her husband near her ever again. She had a very big boy, 9lbs 8ozs. Perhaps that's why. I remember he screamed a lot and she was forever saying be patient, Patrick during breastfeeding and always felt exhausted. He was so demanding. Just like a man, she would say. From womb to tomb.

My friend Jean, mentioned previously, had a lovely baby boy called Dale in June. My school friend, a baby girl called Karen Elisa, a very pretty name. She was a lovely fair-haired baby with dimples and curls. My friend was delighted and a wonderful mother, not that you would have known it. As always her husband knew it all. I always hoped having a daughter, my friend would have an ally against her bully of a husband. Three years later she had a son called Richard. Husband boasting his son and heir, his daughter took second place, like his wife.

I have been writing on. I will now tell you re. my stolen thunder incident – it will be tomorrow, as my fingers are aching, arthritis my constant enemy.

I was being wheeled back to the ward, in a clean nightie, with my case and coat over the end of the stretcher. Tucked up in a cool bed, Sister came and introduced herself and gave congratulations and asked if our baby's name could be put on the end of her crib, other than her surname.

I feel this kind of care is sadly missing in the NHS now and may never return.

She asked me if I would like to telephone my husband to tell him the good news.

She brought the phone unit to my bedside. I telephoned my parents' number as I knew he would be there.

It rang once, my mother answered. I asked for my husband. She said he was doing some shopping for her and would be back in about fifteen minutes. I said I'll ring again.

Before I could close, she said, "Where are you? Have you had your baby?"

I wanted so much to give the news to him. Mummy persisted in answers. I asked her, to please not say anything when he came back. She said I will. I told her briefly that she had a grand-daughter, her weight and birth details, ringing off very dejected. I would ring in fifteen minutes. I was feeling very sleepy, no doubt the effects of anaesthetic. I watched the ward clock. Next, my cheek was being lightly stroked. I woke up and my husband was smiling, said I was the 'cleverest and wonderful girl ever'. He had seen our little girl in the special unit. I said how did you know?

Of course, my mum had told him on his return from shopping and he had come to see me right away, buying me a pearl in a filigree gold case necklace, a baby gold bracelet for his daughter. I was really touched by him saying she was the first person who really belonged to him.

I was so, so disappointed, I started to cry. He comforted me and told me, perhaps there would be another time. I don't know why, but I did not think it would be, so it was my news and I was cross Mummy had stolen my thunder. I never said anything, I just felt resentment. I told a dear friend about the incident, many years later. She said her mother would never let her push the pram when she had her son, practically took over, so it was common. I'm sure parents don't realise and do care. Perhaps it is because their children, they think, never grow up and they know better! It is a learning curve. You have to make many mistakes to mature – I appreciate advice.

I had to stay in hospital three weeks, all but two days. Our baby thrived. She had a lovely shaped head, covered with fine, dark brown hair. To stroke it felt like a peach. Blue eyes for a few days, changing to hazel, her daddy's genes coming through. She was taken to the nursery at night-time, on asking. She was a sleepy girl. This often happens with premature babies. My parents came and looked through the long windows, even brought Bumble to be introduced!

Bringing our little girl home was very special. I did my best to go into a routine – bathing, she was bottle-fed, put out in her pram, either in the porch when it was raining and cold, otherwise in the garden. Every afternoon a walk to the park – choice of three – Bumble alongside, home and tea. In her carrycot for the first four months, always with me, and alongside by our bed at night. She went into her big cot at five months in her own room. The room was in pale lemon, with rabbits playing in sugar almond colours. The curtains were silver threaded on white, with cartoon animals, numerous toys. We gave her a rabbit with a velvet green waistcoat – he was called Snowy. He got lost in our first house move, quickly replaced by another Snowy, pale blue coat this time and she still has him. There was a 'Merrythought' kitten, a poodle, a giraffe, teddy from my parents, countless other little objects, lined up in her cot.

My in-laws were kind, but not particularly enthused. The other son having had a baby girl the year before. He and his new wife lived with them. They had a baby nine months after they were married. In a small maisonette, it was not easy for all of them. His brother was not working and as usual not too concerned. His philosophy was 'something will turn up'. A month after our little girl's arrival, they announced another baby was on the way. Later that year, they moved to Bedford, where his wife came from, to a ground floor flat. They lived there and around for the rest of their lives. They had three children – two girls and a boy. We saw them rarely after the marriage and only heard news through my parents-in-law, who visited them regularly.

Our baby was christened on my birthday, 2nd January, 1961. It was cause for celebration and we had a party at our home. It was a Sunday, so all family and friends could attend. My parents bought her a beautiful christening gown from Harvey Nichols and a matinee jacket of Angora trimmed with velvet. She screamed the devil out of church, unusual as she was a very happy baby. Of course, our life changed and revolved around this little person. She had a wonderful daddy. He would change her, comfort her and any excuse to love her. My parents babysat once a week so we could go out together.

There were no fears re. Bumble. He was interested and sat by me when feeding etc., but did not show any jealousy or aggression, much to my mum's relief. Their relationship later on was so good, she would dress him up, put him in her doll's pram, push him around the garden, and when we went to the shop, he would lay on the end of her pram and a one-sided conversation would take place and I'm sure he understood!

This companionship with animals has, like myself, lasted her into her life and she has always had a dog too, plus a rabbit called 'Edward', after my dad, and when she was five, we bought her a kitten, which she called 'Andrew', a tabby pussycat. He cost 2/6d at a pet shop. He lived eighteen years, outlived Bumble, but later was introduced to my second poodle called 'Pipkin'. Andrew used to sit on the shed roof for a day, I'm sure thinking, she's got another one!

1961 did not have any highlights, except for two events – one sad, one excursion into moving house. In early May, whilst visiting my husband's parents on a Saturday afternoon, my father-in-law was pottering in his small garden. As it often happens, suddenly had a massive coronary and after he was proclaimed dead by ambulance officials, was taken to Wembley Hospital. A terrible shock, as he had always suffered from stomach ulcers, never any indication of heart disease.

My husband was marvellous. Supported his mother in every way, organised the funeral arrangements, informing his seven brothers and sister in Wales. His brother, as usual, sat by. Was sympathetic, but not useful. His mother told me it was relief, not grief. I'm sure in the past there had been affection, but he had browbeaten her all their time together.

They were married in 1927, no more in 1961. Thirty four years.

In June, we thought about moving up the property ladder. We spoke to Mr Warner. He said he would look on the register. He came up very quickly with a detached, four-bedroom house. A doctor's house, who was retiring.

We went to view the house. Again, it was a corner property. Several very good features: oak front and garage doors, a decorative coloured glass landing full-length window. The surgery waiting room was lined in oak and the rooms very light and airy, overlooking a secluded garden. It was off Imperial Way, bordering Harrow and Pinner. We loved it. It did need some updating – a new kitchen and rewiring. It had new gas central heating system and parquet flooring. It was a very elegant house and we knew we could put our stamp on it.

The answer was yes and we immediately put our house on the market and sold it in two weeks. We got a very good price and a smaller mortgage, as the doctor was downsizing to the country and quite happy with our offer. Those were the days when gazumping and people playing games was unheard of and moving house was not as stressful as it is now. This house was and still is one of my favourite homes. We only lived there nine months! That is another episode in my story.

My parents in early September went on a coach holiday to Lucerne in Switzerland. I was so pleased for them, as after the austerity of the war, life was becoming more generous to the middle classes and to people who had always been careful with money. My parents never had HP agreements and paid cash for holidays, furniture, homes etc. They had special occasions to look forward to, as now everyone takes it for granted and think they are entitled, whether they can pay for it or not. Society has changed so dramatically in such a short time.

Whilst my parents were away, my husband went on his annual three day conference, this time in Brighton. He returned on a Friday evening, arrived in time to see his little girl before bedtime. We sat down after our meal and he looked very serious. At the meeting his company had asked him to consider relocating to Newcastle-on-Tyne. He would monitor three depots and staff in Durham, Newcastle and Tyne Tees, with the view of being a Market Director, most likely the duration of five years! My heart sank. I had never been further north than Watford, neither had he for that matter. At least he would have his work and colleagues and I had heard how friendly Geordies were. I would be at home with a small child, a really long way from all my familiar surroundings and my parents. I was so downhearted to say the least and could not take it in. We spoke about it every minute over the weekend. Moving house after such a short time. We did love our new domain. It had been redecorated, a new carpet in the hall and stairs, the central heating was so good. Our little girl seeing her grandparents, going to school, making friends, and dreading telling my parents when they returned.

The three of us went to Victoria Coach Station to meet them.

The journey home was quiet. Mum and Dad did all the talking, still excited about their holiday, how well Mummy had been and all the places they had visited, making a fuss over their grand-daughter and the presents they had in their luggage.

The journey took about forty minutes, back on their own territory and it was about seven-ish and our little girl's bed-time. We suggested they came over to lunch the next day – Sunday. They accepted.

It was a warm day with a soft breeze. Our little girl was just over a year old and walking unsteadily, but adventurously.

We sat in the garden. Telling them then would spoil their lunch, so we waited. In the end I could not contain myself any longer and just said we have something to tell you. A big smile from my dad. I'm sure he thought another baby was on the horizon. Immediately quashed his enthusiasm. We're moving to Newcastle – a promotion and company move! They were both dumbstruck. My mother came to first. We will never see you, we can't come for the day, it's so far, must you go? How long for? My dear dad, even wiped his eye, gave congratulations. We will see each other at every opportunity. When do you have to leave? Are you going to buy a house. So many questions. Of course, we had not even been up to Newcastle as yet. We did not know whether to rent our house in case we moved back. Usually that did not happen, as if and when we moved back, the company's head office was being moved in the near future to Weybridge, Surrey.

The rest of the day we all went around in circles, not solving any of the many dilemmas about the future. Mainly it was the distance – nearly three hundred miles. We might as well have been going to Australia. Needless to say, we sold our house.

In early October 1961, we left our daughter with my parents – for the first time ever – travelled up north. We stayed at the Seaburn Hotel, near Roker Park. The always very cold North East wind was blowing and there were road signs everywhere it seemed, warning of subsidence due to mining. It was a very depressed area and street after street had long terraces of houses, a corner shop and public house. We went to several estate agents in the city. I was not impressed and if you lived across the Tyne, property was very expensive; my husband would be travelling into Yorkshire and south of the Tyne. It was suggested it may be more advantageous to live between Durham and Sunderland, where property varied and there was more countryside. We stayed over a week and eventually found a house at East Herrington. The house was built for the headmaster of Durham University. He was retiring and going to warmer climes. It was at the end of a cul-de-sac of twenty houses, all in different designs, detached, in half an acre of ground, overlooking farmland. The farm was two miles away.

It was a very attractive house; a large front porch leading into a large square hall with a split staircase, with a wrought iron balustrade leading to a large landing, four bedrooms, bathroom, en suite and large bathroom with the bath in the middle, overlooking the terraced garden. The kitchen ran the full length of the back of the house with an inset bay window, again overlooking the garden. It was twenty eight feet long with an AGA. Dining room with the feature of a window seat, large sitting room in the front of the house and large study, which would be a great playroom. The garden had two sets of swings and a slide and sandpit, obviously a family home. It was called Meadow Way.

An offer was made and accepted. The only hiccup, the vendors were leaving in early 1962. Four months away. So in early November we moved into the Seaburn Hotel. My husband's company were very generous – we had a suite and of course Bumble came too. He was spoilt rotten with dinners of chicken and liver and our little girl spoilt by staff. I had a lot of time on my hands and explored our surroundings. The only thing I did not like, it was so very cold. My husband bought me a full length musquash fur coat and often when Bumble went out for a walk, the wind would lift him off the ground. As I had been told, the people were very friendly and always referred to us as from the Capital, which was to us amusing. Many folk had never been to London. I thought that very strange. It was only four hours by train!

The first year we were there my husband's depots won a company award. The reward for the staff was a weekend in a city of their choice. The year before a depot went to Paris. I had high hopes. They chose London. It was like taking coal to Newcastle, excuse the pun. I couldn't believe it. We all came down to London – twenty eight people. We stayed at the London Hilton in Park Lane, went to see the Tower of London, Buckingham Palace, all the usual sites. Went to the theatre. They all thought it was marvellous. To us the norm. An ideal opportunity to see our parents and we left our daughter with them.

As we were not moving until Spring 1962, we spent Christmas at my parents. I stayed on for a further three weeks. Our Harrow house was re-occupied in the autumn.

We moved into Meadow Way in late 1962. We motored up the A1, with our furniture van arriving the next day.

I was glad I had not had to endure the winter there – that was yet to come the following year in 1963, the hardest winter since records began.

My husband knew how lonely I was. There was a scant bus service to Durham and Sunderland and with a pushchair and dog, not easy to travel. He was away a week in every month, visiting depots, training staff and coming down to head office for meetings. Whenever possible, he would take us and I would stay with my parents until he came down again. Fortunately, I made friends with a family living across the way in Meadow Way. They were Geordies. Audrey and Norman. He was an insurer assessor. Audrey stayed at home. They had three children – Pamela, Phillip and Jennifer. Pamela was the nearest in age to our daughter. They were very kind, knowing I was on my own a great deal and I could call on their help at any time and they would be there. They introduced me to northern cuisine and hospitality. We have always kept in touch over the years – Audrey died in 2001. He is now 81. They retired to Winchester, Hampshire. They fell in love with our dog, and poodles, and the first thing they bought was an apricot poodle and now have their second, called Georgie – when they retired. They were the kindest people and filled a big void in my life.

Several of our friends visited us. Jean and David, their son Dale being the same age as our little girl. They now also had another son, Mark, and went onto have a daughter three years later.

Christmas 1962/3, my parents travelled by train to spend the holiday with us.

We met them at Newcastle Station – it was very cold. My mum had a new Astrakhan black coat and a velvet hat. Her pretty silver curly hair, she was still a handsome lady, and my dad had bought a camel hair overcoat. I'm sure they had a premonition of the very, very cold weather yet to come.

Of course we were, like them, so pleased to be together for our first Christmas in the North East. They loved the house. We had all the trimmings and our daughter, who was just over two years old, could take it all in – the lights, Father Christmas, presents, as it is essentially a children's time.

My husband had made her a doll's house. It had carpets, electric light, furniture and was, I thought, a masterpiece. Every detail was well-made. I had contributed by making little crocheted mats for the bedrooms, sheets and covers for the two bedrooms, and a tiny bathroom mat and towels.

In November of that year, my husband's superior in his company, and his wife, had come to stay over whilst visiting the depots. During conversation, they asked us if we would like an Edwardian rocking horse they had in their attic. They had no children and wanted to pass it on to a family. It was very generous and we said our little girl would love it.

It was organised that the horse would be sent up to us from London by train, in time for Christmas. When it arrived it was hidden in next door's garage. They were very nice neighbours – an American who had married an English girl and never gone back to the USA They too had no children, but very friendly and loved our little girl and often had her in their home.

The horse did need some TLC. His tail and mane were in a very sorry state, his leather saddle and the leather things that hold your legs and feet in place (I can't remember the correct names) very worn and not safe.

It was on a solid oak frame and the maker 'Leawood', and a date of making 1905.

My husband set to, went to the nearby farm to obtain real hair for mane and tail. He recovered the saddle with red corduroy, securing it with brass studs. He found a leather maker and renewed the stirrups (I've remembered), polished the oak frame, touched up paintwork. It looked splendid. On Christmas morning, our daughter ran to the horse, never was interested in anything else and sat on it practically all day, even had her breakfast on it. In hindsight, we should have kept the doll's house for her third birthday or Christmas. She loved the horse and not a day went by that she would wide my pony. She talked to him, said goodnight and put a blanket over him at night-time. She would not leave the house without saying bye-bye. It was ridden so fiercely, it would move across the room. Mainly it was in our large hall where there were no obstacles. So much pleasure from that horse, or pony as she called him.

We and our parents had a lovely Christmas and before we could show them our surroundings – Durham Cathedral, Newcastle etc. – on Boxing Day the skies were navy blue and snow was forecast. The weather office was not so efficient as it is now with long-term forecasts.

It started to snow, accompanied by a bitter wind. It snowed, snowed, snowed. Within a week, we were completely housebound, and snowbound. We had a chest freezer to fall on and my dad and husband would walk two miles, taking an hour, over the fields to buy eggs, milk and butter. I had a bread machine and put it to good use. My parents were staying over New Year and to celebrate my twenty-ninth birthday. They had to stay another week, as the south of England almost came to a standstill as the weather was covering the whole country. On Meadow Way, the ice was twelve inches thick on the road and post boxes and telephone kiosks covered in drifts of snow. There were no snow ploughs and every time it snowed, it became more and more impacted. The children built igloos and got a lot of fun out of the situation. No one could get to work, shops did not open, buses and trains stopped. It was chaos. As always, with us Brits, when our backs are to the wall, we excel. We helped each other and made the best of it. The weather lasted well into early March. It was a real challenge. I wondered if we had to look forward to four more winters like this. Time would tell…

1963

By the end of March, the awful weather began to improve. The spring in the North East is always later.

I was getting used to living in East Herrington, always aware how far away it was from my roots. I was, as I have said before, fortunate to have the opportunity to visit my parents every six weeks. My husband suggested we planned a holiday in Denmark. We would go from Parkeston Quay, near Harwich, by ship and then go by train across the islands to Springforbi, forty minutes north of Copenhagen.

The hotel overlooked the inland sea and on a clear day you could see Sweden. In the winter it froze over and you could skate or walk across. Springforbi was a health resort with special properties in the water. The people were charming and very pro-British. We had a sitting-room-come-bedroom, with a sledge bed for our daughter. There was a very good train service to Copenhagen and we went many times. It was June and good weather. All the clientele were Danish. We were made so welcome and nothing was too much trouble. They catered for our every whim, especially our little girl's meals. If you asked for a soft boiled egg and soldiers, that is exactly what you got.

Denmark is very soft, green, undulating in scenery, like I thought in England. No mountain range, wood-built houses in the countryside and apartments in the cities. We went several times to the Tivoli Gardens which was enchanting. Very good presentation and so much to see. Nothing looked cheap and the cleanliness was outstanding. If you did drop anything, you were quietly reminded that there are refuse bins everywhere, which are emptied several times a day – a lesson for us, I think. They are very proud of their environment. Are we? Proud I mean.

We visited Elsinore of course, Hamlet and William Shakespeare very evident.

We had a great holiday and I have often thought I would like to go again, to see if it is the same as in my memory.

Another treat came about later in the year – we went to Venice, Italy.

My parents were going by coach. Dad still had reservations about flying for Mummy. They wanted us to come and we would all celebrate our daughter's third birthday on 29th August.

In Venice they had doll shops and although our little girl was not doll mad, my parents wanted to buy her a doll.

On her special day, we sat and had coffee in St Mark's Square, whilst they, the three of them, went off for her present.

I must admit she looked sweet, wearing a white Broderie Anglais, Mr Magoo sun hat, a pink dress I had smocked across the bodice, white shoes and socks. She was a stocky little girl, always smiling and friendly and obviously English. We took photographs, especially the pigeons sitting on her hat, shoulders and arms. She showed no fear whilst tourists took photographs too.

They returned with the precious doll – not to my taste, considering she could have chosen any doll in the shop! Her name was 'Poldina'. She had a smock top on over frilly knickers. She was called a 'floppy doll', something new, evidently, looking like a real baby – the surprise was, she had a Mongolian face. She loved that doll and still has Poldina forty seven years later.

No words can describe the magic of Venice, and Italy became my favourite holidays. I like the Italian attitude to life – enjoy, the respect for their elderly folk and family life. I know their economics are always questionable! I like the outstanding history, painting and art, and they have outstanding style in furniture, jewellery, décor and clothes, plus they are such a good-looking race – I have a penchant for dark, curly hair, hence my husband's attraction to me.

On our return back to East Herrington, and foreboding re. another North East winter, a surprise was in store.

In late September 1963 my husband's conference came around. It was being held in London for the first time. It gave me the opportunity to visit my parents. The event always finished on a Friday, so we would return to the North East on Sunday. We travelled on the A1 (no motorway at that time). It took approximately nearly five hours. During this time, I always visited my mum-in-law. She was still living in her small maisonette. My brother-in-law was now living in Rushden, Bedfordshire, and was yet again expecting another babe. Mum was convinced they would go on until a boy arrived. My mother-in-law had no friends and was very lonely and isolated. This was mainly due to her lack of confidence. She just would not make the effort, which was sad and such a waste of life.

My husband arrived about four-ish, smiling, smiling. I thought he had news of a salary increase and promotion!

Tea was made and he could not contain his good news. We were moving back south. Everything was going so well in the North East and so my husband would be made a Marketing Director and would still travel in and around the South of England, but permanently based in Weybridge, head office. I do not know whether I was numb with delight or mentally thinking, golly, moving again. Our fourth move and house since we had been married. I was so happy. Our little girl could start the nearby school, make long-time friends and most of all, as had been discussed many times, we would have another baby. My husband had been reluctant whilst we lived in the north, as it was intimated I would have the same complication as before and he wanted me to be near my parents.

We drove back to East Herrington on a high. We put our house on the market and decided to wait until we were in the south again, staying with my parents, before we made our move to Surrey. My husband moved into head office before New Year 1964.

We would, of course, be able to leave our girlie with my parents whilst we looked for another home. Prices had increased since we left Pinner. Surrey was a very upmarket area. In March 1964 we saw a small estate being built in Bagshot. Waterers Nursery had sold off some land, just off the A30, surrounded by woodland. There was one house left and we liked it very much and put down a deposit. Once again, a corner house, number eleven Lambourne Drive. We moved in late May 1964. Although I had a very pleasant time in the North East, when we drove out of Meadow Way for the last time, I did not look back.

Settling in and getting to know your neighbours and surroundings always takes time. I found having a small child and a dog rarely goes unnoticed and people with like soon chat to you when out and about. The surrounding properties were also occupied by young married couples, either with children or starting out in their first homes.

My husband knew the area very well as he had been stationed in Blackdown Barracks during his National Service and cycled every weekend past the bottom of the road we now lived in to see me during our courtship. Camberley in one direction, one and a half miles, and Sunningdale in the opposite way on the A30.

Later in the autumn, we made enquiries re. a school for our little girl. She was due to start school in September 1965. In those days there were very few nursery schools and most mums stayed at home to be with their little ones. Something I feel very strongly about, as children's formative years are the most important. When you have a child you must, I think, dedicate sixteen years of your life to their upbringing and welfare. This support gives dividends later in life. The family unit is now practically non-existent and children are emotionally neglected and this, once gone, can never be replaced or repaired.

We had discussed and decided to send her to a convent school. Really my influence here, as I was very happy during my school life in this environment. No pressure and calm reigns in convent schools and the nuns dedicated to their charges. No worries re. home life and finance and 'keeping up with the Joneses', just looking after the children in their care.

There was a sister convent, linked to mine, in Sunninghill called 'The Marist' – no longer there, I'm sorry to say. (I've learnt they are still there.) You could stay through from five to eighteen years and I think the stability and friendships you form stay with you through life. Children like to feel security and stability and love in their lives and later in this manuscript it was proved over and over again to me with young people I supported through the Crown Court Witness Service. I will relate in detail later in this writing.

We wrote to Reverend Mother requesting an interview. Of course, we received a reply. It was on a Saturday morning. We were ushered into a private room with a long refectory table.

Reverend Mother was a small lady, with the serene face and manner that nuns seem to have. She was interested in my convent background and how happy I was at a similar school. She focused her attention on our little girl, who behaved well and answered all her questions. She invited us to look around the junior school and said on leaving she would be writing in due course. Later that week a letter arrived, saying she would be pleased to welcome our child to the school in the autumn of 1965, details of uniform requirements, times of attendance and fees.

In late 1964, my parents were now seriously contemplating their retirement in the following year. They had decided to move to Hampshire. It was a county they knew well and also they had friends who had lived there many years.

They had seen a small development of bungalows in a village called Stubbington, a mile from Lee-on-Solent and a few miles from Fareham, between Portsmouth and Southampton. The road link was good for the motorway and was now in operation which would make a journey of approximately one and a quarter hours to visit us and friends they still had in and around their old home in Wembley.

The bungalow chosen was in a cul-de-sac of six on the edge of the village, which consisted of a grocery and greengrocery/butchers and a newsagents, church, and of course a public house. Not too near the sea, which ruins your property with the salt atmosphere. It was very flat, which was ideal for my mother. The bungalow was detached, two bedrooms, kitchen/diner, bathroom and a large sitting room with bay window overlooking the long front garden. The front door was on the side of the bungalow. A detached garage and a rear garden which was grassed with mandatory flower beds and my dad's favourite yellow roses called 'Golden Showers' which were grown on the side of the garage. They were not overlooked as the land at the rear was Ministry of Defence naval land and was an acreage and would not be built on. It was maintained regularly and just looked like a meadow, access between the bungalows. It was called Tangyes Close. My parents did not realise at the time, when you live in a cul-de-sac you only see the people living there and when my mother was left alone, I know she felt very isolated and missed very much passing traffic and people, as we lived near the Uxbridge tube line and they were always seeing people and neighbours previously. Something I have always kept in mind, as when you are older and especially on your own, it is very important for stimulation and loneliness which is a disease all of its own with elderly folk.

My parents moved in early June 1965. Four months before my dad's retiring birthday.

I went to help with packing up thirty years of living in the same home. I felt very nostalgic, even sad, knowing I would not be visiting my first home with so memories – all good. Wartime, the Morrison Shelter in the front room – sleeping in and used as an eating table, doing homework, a place for Christmas trees, presents, a velour tablecloth to hide what it really was, a buffet table for parties. I cannot remember when it was discarded, obviously when the air raids were no more. Sitting in the same room, before television, listening to the radio, playing cards, and records on a wind up machine and more importantly, talking about what was going on around us. Family matters, financial and personal. If you were lucky, maybe a holiday and whether you could save up for a car. My dad always spent his holidays painting the house and general DIY, taking a day out to the seaside now and again. My parents went to the Derby at Epsom every year on a double decker bus, always hoping for a winner and my mum was usually the lucky one. She had a great memory for form and never came away with more money than she left with.

In the packing, boxes of photographs that I rescued and at a later date put names and dates to faces and made up albums. Many neighbours called in to say au revoir and reminisced of time gone by.

All three of us verbally said goodbye to our house, as the removal van moved away.

I have been back there to have a look, after my parents had died. Of course it is not the same and a friend several years ago sent me a cutting showing our house – sold for £183,000 in the 1980s. My parents bought it for £300 in 1935. They would have been flabbergasted. They sold it for £32,000.

They were staying overnight with us in Bagshot as their furniture was arriving the next day. A new adventure for them and a different journey for me, their daughter. (I add another paragraph here that I must describe. I will staple to this page – our little girl started school in September 1966.)

We moved house for the fifth time.

I was finding it heavy going, as was our daughter, going back and forth to school. We walked over two miles each way, in all weathers. We saw the house which was built in a private park, the corner of the park, sold off some land, for eight detached houses. We called our new home 'Leawood' which was very appropriate as the gardens were established with silver birches, Rhododendrons and Azaleas fully grown, and each house had gardens of a quarter of an acre and were each built so not overlooked by their neighbours. The house had four bedrooms, a playroom/study, large kitchen, combined lounge/dining room with a stone central fireplace to both rooms, double garage and car port. This house was, I always regarded, my favourite house. The surroundings were beautiful in a pretty village of Windlesham, between Bagshot and Sunningdale and on the edge of Chobham Common. We lived there nearly twenty years of happiness, sadness, that all families experience in life.

After moving in early April, I also decided with persuasion from my husband and Dad to learn to drive!

My dad and Mummy regularly visited as they now had their own time to enjoy. On every visit my dad took me out in his car. He had patience personified. The light evenings made it possible for me to practice every evening, with my husband the other instructor. He too was patient, but unlike my dad said very little and when I asked him why, he said he was petrified as I became very adventurous in the driving seat, which was against my nature. I thought that very amusing at the time. Many years later he admitted I was a very good driver and never broke the rules or took a chance. After four months my dad suggested I had six lessons with BSM to give me some polish and iron out any bad habits my instructors may have overlooked. I enrolled – the lessons were fifty pence per hour! 10/-. I applied for my test. It was at Guildford. It was a very rainy day at twelve noon, late October. I passed my test with flying colours and my dear dad as a reward promptly bought me a Fiat 800 Operto, wine colour. It was my pride and joy.

The journey to school was solved and I found independence and wished I had learnt to drive earlier in life. Everything in my life was rewarding, happy, the still kindest, caring husband, a lovely little girl and my parents happy in their new environment, still hoping for another baby and in 1967 it happened. Unfortunately, not a happy outcome. I'll relate as there were other events in 1967 that were both happy and also very worrying. So into 1967 we go.

In April, my parents celebrated their Ruby wedding. It was planned by them, as a small dinner party. We had other ideas and unbeknown to them, we contacted their bridesmaid and her husband who was their best man. Mummy's two sisters were invited, only as we knew, one accepted – my auntie who I mentioned lived in Gibraltar previously – six close friends, my husband, me and our little girl.

I felt it was appropriate, considering they met and married in three weeks and were happy for forty eight years. My dad was so caring and attentive, as my mother's health was always fragile. They were a very grounded couple, not covetous or discontented, living through the war, liked their home and surroundings, and now able to enjoy well-earned retirement.

The evening went so well and was a complete surprise to them. Everyone was happy and although the British are not great communicators, the company chatted and laughed as if all the years melted away.

In July, I knew I was expecting another babe – due I was told to arrive in late February 1968. Needless to say, we were over the moon. We told our parents, not our daughter, until I knew all was well. In hindsight, maybe I had a premonition. In September, my husband was going to the United States for two and a half months. His company wanted feedback re. marketing on frozen foods in the USA. Travelling New York/middle west across country to San Francisco and returning home mid-December 1967.

This would be the first time we had been apart since our marriage and although I was apprehensive, I had the responsibility of the most important little person in our lives and I knew my parents would give me all their support.

I was having a much better time in this pregnancy; no ongoing sickness and I had plenty of energy. My weight gain was under scrunity, almost nil. We all went to Heathrow to say farewell. My husband promised to write every day, as in times gone by, and cards to our little girl and phone calls to hear her voice. He left on a Friday so the first weekend was the hardest. No one to intimately talk to and discuss issues. I felt mature enough to deal with events and there was always the wisdom of my dad.

The usual routine continued – taking the school run and activities, piano lessons and out-of-school events. My husband arrived safely and was immediately wined and dined by the generous Americans. He was invited by colleagues to their homes as the English are always made welcome with their cultural background and allies of America. Letters were interesting and he could not get over the food that was consumed – breakfast, brunch, lunch and dinner. Also the sheer size of the USA against our small island. After two weeks into his trip, suddenly letters and phone calls stopped. At first I thought he could be travelling around, tiredness. It was so unusual, no contact. After six days I rang his office here in the UK. They too were concerned, not alarmed, promising to look into his itinerary and his whereabouts. I heard nothing for two days. His superior telephoned and very gently told me my husband was in a private hospital in Modesto, California.

The information was he was paralysed in his legs and tests were taking place. He was reluctant to tell me due to pregnancy and being so far away. His telephone number was made available on my insistence and due to the time difference, I waited until after 10:30 p.m. and made the call.

I had told my parents and they immediately came up from Hampshire to be with me. It goes without saying, I was very frightened. He had never been unwell, except for mild asthma when a child.

On telephoning, a wait, which seemed forever. I was transferred to his room in the hospital.

After tears on both sides, he assured me he was okay and explained he felt ill on the flight from Chicago to Los Angeles and on checking into his hotel, went to bed, thinking jet lag was the reason. He woke up after six hours and tried to get out of bed and fell on the floor. He rang the desk, their service was instant. They called an ambulance and after formalities of insurance etc., he was admitted to hospital. The American system is different to ours. They test everything from top to toe, whereas we go to the source of illness and take decisions from there. He related he could not stand, shower or do anything for himself and he just did not know whether he would continue to be in this state and did not know if it was going to be ongoing, which frightened him very much. I asked if I could speak to a consultant. He was very sympathetic and assured me everything would be done to help my husband and he would keep in touch. I promised my husband I would telephone him at the same time every day.

I also spoke to our doctor and asked him if he would talk to his American counterpart, as medics communicate to each other and keep relatives on the perimeter, giving reassurance which although caring, leaves one very frustrated and imagining all manner of things.

After another seven days of no definite news, my dad said he would travel out to the USA. A great gesture. I telephoned his office and said re. this decision and they said they would do everything to help; arrange visa and travelling documents.

When I next spoke to my husband, he said that would be marvellous, but he would dismiss himself from hospital and come home with assistance. He spoke to his company with this suggestion and they agreed he had a nurse accompany him to New York. British Airways would take seats out to accommodate the stretcher and on arrival at Heathrow, an ambulance would take him to a hospital in Ravenscourt Park, London. He just did not want my dad to be alone in the USA and plus, he really felt coming home and our doctors would help his condition, and having his family around him.

I have omitted to say, my father-in-law died in 1962. His funeral took place from our home in Pinner, a few months before we left to live in the North East. His mother became very reclusive. When I told her re. my husband's health, she made no comment and although on his return to the UK he was in hospital four months, she never visited him, although I assured her I would take her by car and please come and stay as long as she liked. Her home was six stops on the underground. It was sad, but as always he never said. Very hurtful to me and not understandable to anyone.

My husband's condition did not deteriorate, just stayed the same. No use in his legs and various infections. The consultant was mystified, felt he had something wrong in one of his filter organs, tonsils/kidneys. Every test was done and by a process of elimination, they found something amiss with his spleen. After more investigations, treatment was intensive with injections, antibiotics, physio. He started to improve and within three weeks was carefully walking with crutches twice a day. The doctors never gave his condition a proper medical name, assured us he would make a full recovery, given time and patient patience.

His company were very good and took work into the hospital; reports, statistics etc., and told him he was only to return when he was 100% well.

During this time, I had been having check-ups. In the sixties there were no ultrasounds for expectant mothers. It was left to your doctor and pre-natal visits to the hospital. I had been advised to have a caesarean section in view of the past pregnancy.

I awoke. It was a Thursday. My parents were still staying and every day after collecting our daughter from school, we, my dad and I would motor approximately fifty minutes to visit my husband. On this Thursday, I asked my dad if he would go on his own. I felt very unwell and had pains in my abdomen. I got up, but very quickly returned to bed with a hot water bottle. I was unable to sleep because of pain.

By early afternoon, my mother's insistence, the doctor arrived. He was a lovely man – Pakistani, who had studied medicine at Barts Hospital, married an English nurse and settled in Woking and been our doctor for three years.

He examined me and said he wanted me admitted to hospital. I was five months' pregnant and as far as I was concerned, all was well. Alarm bells started ringing in my head. Please, not after all this time, nothing must go wrong.

At this time, my husband's illness was paramount and had been since his return from the USA. Again, little did either of us know there were going to be changes in our life, especially for my husband.

I was taken to hospital by ambulance. Events happened very quickly. I was made ready for theatre, constantly assured by staff, as my only concern was my baby. It would be four months early!

I woke up in a darkened room, a nurse by the bedside. I was very sleepy, of course, and asked many times if my baby was alright. The nurse said the doctor would come tomorrow and try and rest. Although I'm sure everyone wants to believe all is well, I just knew. Everything was all wrong.

The next day was not a good day.

The surgeon came to see me approximately 8:30 a.m. to put me out of my misery. I had lost my baby. I had an ectopic pregnancy which as I did not know was a baby in the fallopian tube. He advised me I was very fortunate, as usually they occur early in pregnancy and I was nearly five months. He had had to remove the tube and he said it was highly unlikely I would conceive again, and certainly not without problems.

He tried to console me, that I had one perfect little girl and sometimes nature decides these events and nothing to blame myself for, it just sometimes happens.

I was heartbroken and tried to take the positive view that another baby may be possible. I was so miserable and when my parents came in to see me, kept telling me it was for the best and get well as my husband would be coming home soon. I thought he may blame himself – the stress I had been under. I spoke to other doctors and nurses and they assured me, it was a mishap of reproduction and can happen to anyone. My dad went to see my husband and told him and immediately my husband rang and reassured me with loving words and said I must get well and we would be home together soon, with our daughter.

I recovered from the operation, but was left with haemorrhaging that did not last weeks, went into months and months. I became very anaemic. My energy levels were nil. I did not want to go out, plus now my husband was home on crutches. I felt constantly tired, every day resting and in bed at 8:00 p.m. My doctor was marvellous and after six months of iron injections, two blood transfusions, sent me to a specialist, who recommended I had a complete hysterectomy. I was devastated. He told me to go home, discuss it with my husband. His last remark, saying I could not get pregnant in this present state and the haemorrhaging could continue indefinitely and that just was not good.

I did just that. Talked and talked over with my husband, my parents and they said the decision was mine, but my health was the most important issue and I could not continue in this way.

I decided I would try and hold on for a further six months and if nothing changed, I would have the op, as advised.

Nothing did change. In fact, it worsened, and one day when I was feeling very low, I telephoned my doctor and asked him to put the wheels in motion. I entered the Nuffield Hospital in Woking, knowing my baby days were over. I was just thirty six.

I must admit, I felt so much better and within six weeks, back to normal, driving, taking our girlie to school. My husband was driving again and going into his office, three days a week, and after five months, back as before.

Around the corner was yet another blow, this time my dad. My wise, lovely dad. Always in my corner and only two and a half years into his well-deserved retirement.

Both my mother and ourselves noticed changes, only slight at first, of behaviour, not listening and forgetfulness, being disorientated, especially when outside of his surroundings. My mum said it was age. He was coming up sixty nine.

My dad seemed totally unaware of the situation. When we suggested he spoke to his doctor, he laughed. He wasn't as young as he used to be and not to worry. I could only remember him having the flu or lumbago. He was the stronger, health-wise, than my mum.

One Saturday, early evening, the telephone rang. It was my mother, very distressed. My dad had climbed out of the window, saying he must go to work.

We got into the car and in record time, arrived at my parents' home.

My mother had persuaded my dad to come in and he was rambling and very disturbed. After reassurance, a cup of tea, we suggested he rest. He was childlike and yet belligerent if he did not agree. All three of us agreed the doctor must be called. He was in the bungalow in twenty minutes. A Dr. Duncan, in his forties, with a soft Scots accent. He went into the bedroom, we stood at the door. He was kind, gentle, asked my dad many questions about the past. He answered correctly, but recent events he could not remember at all.

He gave my dad a sedative and came and sat in the kitchen. He was making arrangements for my dad to be admitted to Southampton General for tests and a lobotomy. He left saying to telephone immediately if my dad's condition changed and we would hear from him on Monday morning re. his admittance to hospital.

All day Sunday Dad was quiet, uninterested in food, as if he was in a far place. My mother was convinced he had had a stroke and once in hospital, we would know what was going on.

My husband and daughter returned home late on Sunday evening by train, leaving me with a car to take my mum to Dad on Monday. Southampton was half an hour away. Duly on Monday the doctor was as good as his word. I picked up a letter en route to Southampton. We arrived at the hospital. My dad was very amenable and we assured him he would feel better and would be well looked after and we would be back later that day. It was a very modern hospital and everyone was helpful and caring.

My mum had had a bad asthma attack that morning and was exhausted, so I suggested we return to their home and Mummy rested. It was foolish to say the usual expletives. She was so worried and stress always affected her condition.

Mummy was so breathless and unwell, I went on my own to see Dad. This happened in the following years, as Mummy's health reverted back to the early years; an attack every day, and more sometimes, that left her exhausted, with little or no energy. Sometimes she could hardly speak she was so breathless and wheezy. Adrenaline injections came back into her life. She could not walk very far and going on a bus was out of the question.

My dad was in hospital a week. On the following Friday, we went to visit. He looked the same, greeted us in his usual tactile way, as if he had not seen us for months. At the end of our visit, the doctor asked us to come to his room. We felt quite upbeat. Dad had not had any further symptoms and we wanted it to be a 'blip' and my dad was with us again.

The doctor came around and put his arm around my mother and held my hand and told us awful news! My dad had senile dementia, better known these days as Alzheimer's disease.

In the late sixties this condition was rarely spoken of and little known by the general public as it is today.

As with all bad news, you don't believe it. Your loved one will get better and after a while you know it is not true and somehow you have to get through it. I realise now how hard it was for my mother, as mental problems, through ignorance, was a terrible taboo and never discussed. The doctor gave us a rundown on how it would progress, which left us distraught and a great feeling of hopelessness.

He explained my dad's motor regions would fail – not walking and speaking, childlike sometimes and difficult. His memory would become non-operative, not even remembering who we were. He gave us a life expectancy of approximately three years, if he continued to go downhill.

He would deteriorate and then level off and the illness could accelerate. He assured us there was no cure and that eventually he would die. There was no medication. As I said, hopelessness.

My poor mother was traumatised and I was doubly worried re. her always fragile health. She had never been alone and always cared for by my dad. It's nothing new. Life can be so cruel and unfair. I wonder why?

For the next five and a half years my life was one of travelling seventy miles, picking up my mother and going back fifteen miles to visit my dad in a home. Mummy had him home from hospital. After four months, his behaviour became more and more unpredictable and with the doctor's help, he was found a place in a home near West Wickham, Hampshire. There was no bus service from my parents' village, so of course I knew my mother would fret if she could not see him. I journeyed down four times a week and in bad weather I would stay over. My mother didn't mean to, she became very demanding and thought my duty was paramount and constantly told me, I would still be young when it was all over. Occasionally, Daddy came home for a weekend. It was always worrying. He would climb out of the window and all manner of different situations would arise and in the end, there was no alternative but for him to stay in the home permanently.

My husband was, as always, understanding and gave me support and so good with our daughter. Friends rallied around and were very kind and supportive. I never seemed to be in my own home more than two days and in the car, towards my parents' home to pick up Mummy, or if she was not well enough, visit my dad alone.

Although I had come to terms with my dad's illness, it was very distressing to see someone you love very much turn into someone else, who did not know you and was in a world of his own. With us in body, but not in spirit.

Believe me when I say I wanted to see him. He seemed not to know I was his daughter and Mummy his wife, just two kind ladies who came to see him and there were many times when he would comment that his wife had died years ago, all part of his dementia. He was never sad or distressed, always managed a smile and childlike in his attitude and although after visiting, usually for two hours, my mother would wave and say see you soon, he turned away without any recognition or recollection we had been there. This upset my mother more than anything else, that he was not aware of us in his life. My mother never came to terms with his dementia and would often say, I think Daddy was better today, and I would nod in agreement. There was no point in doing otherwise.

My life seemed to revolve around this situation and the strain of it all took its toll. I developed a stomach ulcer. The outcome was surgery, I'll relate about later. Although the doctor said his life expectancy was approximately two to three years, years went by... four, five. My dad was a fit man, in good physical health. He never lost his hair, was upright and didn't seem to age outwardly. He had a vacant look and showed no interest in anything.

In early 1975, my dad had been in the home nearly six years. On a visit, he was walking with a limp and both my mother and I asked the staff if he could see the doctor, who called into the home twice a week.

The doctor sent him to Southampton Hospital for an X-ray and it was revealed he had fractured his hip. He had said nothing and we didn't ever really know how this injury had occurred. Maybe a fall. The staff could not be with each and every one. All the patients were in different stages of dementia and would wander around, going in cupboards and moving in their rooms.

The hospital admitted him and he had surgery — not a new hip, a pinning was done to stabilise the bone. I am quite willing to admit, I really hoped he would not recover from surgery and that God would take him home, so that he would not suffer anymore.

He was sitting up in bed, looking like his old self. His teeth in, his hair combed and the extra bonus. As I came into the ward, his face lit up and he waved and when sitting by his bed, said, It's lovely to see my 'best girl', something he always called me when growing up. I thought there had been a miracle. Maybe the anaesthetic had cleared his brain. It was short-lived as the next day, with my mother, we visited and he was in a cot bed so that he could not fall out of bed, back to the other Dad, not knowing who we were. I never told my mother about my previous visit. She would have been so distressed or maybe his recognition of her, just once more.

After a few days, my dad was put in a room with fans going and constant nursing. It was about ten days after his surgery, a Saturday, February 22nd. I had been staying with Mum and decided to go home and return the next day with my husband. I left my parents' home at 9:30 a.m. and en route, as I was passing the hospital, a quick visit to see my dad and continue on my journey home.

I went into his room. He looked very ill. His lovely China blue eyes were paler and he was obviously running a temperature. The doctor came in and I said, Do you think my dad will come through? He said, Who knows. He is very, very ill, my dear. I held his hand and kissed him and left for Surrey.

I returned home by 2:30 p.m.-ish, did some shopping, went to see our daughter who was staying with a friend. Lots of hugs which buoyed me up and I returned to my home. It was a lovely sunny day – cold, but very pleasant, blue skies. I wished all was right with my world.

I made a cup of tea. The telephone started to ring. I answered. A soft voice asked me if I was alone. I lied. I almost knew what I was going to be told. Your father died ten minutes ago. It was 3:14 p.m. I asked them not to telephone my mother as she would be alone. She always rang the hospital at 5:00 p.m. I said I would motor down to her by that time and I would tell her. They were very understanding and said they would see me the following day.

During the years of my dad's ill health, my husband had left Birds Eye. This decision was made through different issues, since his illness in the USA. The three day week had transpired, we were in Ted Heath's government. My husband seemed to be constantly in his car, never getting anywhere fast, plus he felt his ambitions were in a tunnel. After many talks, he decided to go into business on his own. My dad had always said he would do well, plus the moving around was not what we wanted. It was hinted it was going to happen in the near future, uprooting our daughter. We wanted to put down some roots. Moving house is not easy for all concerned. Making new friendships and so on and so forth. He bought a leasehold property – a shop in Station Road, Aldershot, eleven miles from our home. It had a floor area of a small Smith's. He sold newspapers over the counter and mainly paperback books, Parker pens, leather goods, selected cards, wrapping paper etc.

He worked in head office for eighteen months to make sure it flourished, employing an excellent manageress. It was a great success. Very good passing clientele en route to the station, army personnel, and opposite the general Post Office. He opened at 7:45 a.m., closing at 6:00 p.m., and closed on Sundays. He gave up his post at Birds Eye and concentrated on his business in Aldershot, in his mind that maybe if all went well, he would buy another business.

After receiving the saddest news re. my dad, I telephoned him. He said he would come down to be with my mother and myself.

I got in the car, the second time that day. I wanted to be at my parents' home before my mother rang the hospital. I drove faster than usual, stopping only for petrol in Farnham. The sun was out – a cold day and one of the saddest for me. I turned into the cul-de-sac. My mother's sitting room was in the front of their home. She came out of the door. I knew she knew why I was there. The date, February 22nd, 1975. My lovely first dog died the next day.

My dad's funeral did not take place in the usual seven days. The hospital requested the coroner for an inquest to affirm how my dad's hip fracture had occurred.

The inquest was at Southampton ten days later. My mother was unable to attend due to stress and a constant asthma condition. Me, being the next of kin, attended. My husband accompanied me.

I was assured it was only a formality. One of the good laws of the United Kingdom.

All went well and it was given he died of after effects of his operation, plus a perforated bowel. The home was completely exonerated and we left knowing cremation arrangements could be arranged. My dad had left details of all arrangements, to make it as easy as possible for my mother.

Portchester Crematorium was the nearest crematorium and the date and time were 8th March at 12 noon. Three hundred people attended – colleagues and friends from way back. My parents' bungalow was bulging. Always saying what a special person my dad was. I didn't need to have that confirmed, I knew, and I still miss him every day, after thirty six years.

We took my mother home and my husband talked about a holiday later in the year. During the next years, my mamma did not cope well with widowhood. She had never had to live on her own. When young her family had cosseted her, due to her health, and also my dad when they married and through their life together.

Mamma would come and stay in November and leave in February, the Christmas holiday, and again in March through to the beginning of May, the Easter, and I always went down to be with her two or three times a week during the interim times. I suggested she join groups. She was a great card player and a very gregarious person, but she just wasn't a joiner and her bungalow became a prison to her. She had two personal friends and occasionally would visit them. They usually visited her. Winters were the bad times and became the norm. She asked to come and stay with us.

I bought another poodle – he was called 'Pipkin'.

Please do not misunderstand me. I loved my mum dearly, but I too had nearly six years of caring about Dad, with no let up and now I felt more than helpless dealing with my mum's emotions. I had developed a duodenal ulcer and seemed to be always at the doctor's.

Things came to a head in 1978 when I had radical surgery. I have was told later a vagotomy operation. The operation is no longer in place. I was in hospital four weeks. Also at this time, our daughter no longer lived at home, sharing a house with her friend, whilst training and taking her City & Guilds in all aspects of hairdressing, wig making and hair design. I felt very isolated and missed my daughter very much, as a confidant. I realise now that my husband was not good at confrontation. He knew what a worrier I was, sometimes without foundation. Generally I would have liked him to reassure me that my fears were unfounded. Have some space from my mother's demands. I seemed to juggle my time between my mother seventy miles away and worrying re. my daughter, who I did not see very often. I felt my husband's attitude was anything for a quiet life. He was a peacekeeper. Just sometimes I wanted him to make a difference.

I also confided in my mum's sisters. They lived far away and always invited my mother to visit. Mum would go as long as I did the driving to and from. One in Plymouth and the more sympathetic aunt lived in Harrow (my Gibraltar auntie mentioned before in my narrative).

My mother's eldest sister had lived with her daughter all her life. Again, a very demanding lady, who considered it was your duty to give 95% of your time to a parent, irrespective if you had a husband and family. I'm sure many, daughters especially, have this in their lives and that's why their relationships suffer and people grow apart, without realising it's happening. When the obvious happens and your parent dies, you are left with a void you cannot resolve. I do not wish to dwell on this time. I made a life-long resolve never to put my daughter in the same place. As later in my narrative you will read, I have been alone over twenty years. I remember this time and hope I am not in the same place. I'm very sure my mother did not realise. She was desperately lonely and I always feel people must find an interest and seize the day – it is not disrespectful to your parent. It makes the battleground of life easier to bear.

At a dinner party, a gentleman I had met before, he was the husband of a lady who was chairman of a private ladies' club, I was a member. He asked me if I had ever given some thought in becoming a magistrate. I replied, never. I thought like most members of the public, you had to know about laws of the land.

The conversation re. magistrate went from my mind. I did not even mention it to my husband. I bought yet another dog, a standard apricot – a Poodle called 'Tweed'.

Great unrest in the country due to the Labour party trying to keep wages down. Our business was thriving and my husband took me on holiday to Israel – I was very impressed how the country had developed. We did the tourist thing, Eilat, through the Negev Desert to Masada, Dead Sea and Jerusalem. Our travel company was first class re. travelling and hotels etc., usually. Except one of the most horrendous and yet very enjoyable journeys I have had, which I will now recall. It is indelible in my mind and remembering always leaves a smile.

We went down to the reception area in our hotel. It had the grand name of the 'Queen of Sheba'. There were two people from South Wales on a world trip, complete with twelve pieces of luggage and a full-length mink coat!

Two gay lads from Morocco, a pretty nun, visiting the Holy Land, and what turned out to be the character of the journey, a large Dutch lady, smiling and very friendly.

When we all introduced ourselves, her first words, "If we have the British on board, we will be fine". She would put her arm around you and say, "I like the British – good people, always compassionate and fair, and very clever".

We were waiting for, we had been told, a stretch limousine with air conditioning which would be very pleasant, as it was in high thirties. We were beckoned outside and there it was – definitely a stretch limousine – no windows, so I guess you could say air-conditioned, bullet holes all over the place. We reckoned it had been in the 'Six-Day War'. The interior left a lot to be desired. The boot was tied up with string, not a good omen for Eileen's luggage and only six seats for seven. A smiling Arab was the driver, did not speak English. He had very brown teeth and some missing, due to chewing betel nuts on a regular basis.

We all were dismayed, but were assured the journey to Jerusalem would only take four and a half hours and it was a nice day. Ha ha.

The two gay lads sat on the bench seat at the rear with me stretched out on their laps. The lovely Dutch lady in a single seat, in front of me and the lads. Eileen and Arthur on another bench seat, with the nun in front and my husband sitting alongside the driver. The driver treated the gears as if it was a tank, which made you wince and had no respect for what was once upon a time a great car. It was a Mercedes and a great car by reputation. Our luggage together with remaining cases went on the roof and Eileen never left her coat anywhere, always over her arm. I always carried a damp flannel and tangerines for some fluid intake and before we had left Eilat, I handed them around. Eileen had a bottle of water and I did not ask the lads, but I think it was alcohol. They held hands and seemed to talk very fast in their language. The serene nun was calm in personality, as they always appear to be, and I asked her wasn't she hot with her habit on, to which she replied: "It keeps the heat out and I'm used to it." The Dutch lady was bursting out of her cotton dress. I guessed she may be wearing corsets and that must be so uncomfortable in that heat. She never, never complained and would pat my arm whenever I asked if she was okay, and out would come more praise of the British.

The desert was not a bit like I imagined – boulders and like dumped building refuse – and every so many miles, a sign, saying there could be flash floods and people die of drowning as well as lack of water.

Occasionally, you would have sand dunes on either side of our car track. We tried to enquire, how long would the journey take. Each and every one of us had a different answer and the driver just grinned. We had left our hotel at 9:20 a.m. and after two and a half hours, we made the driver understand we wanted to stop. After about twenty minutes, we came upon what appeared to be an army encampment and that's exactly what it was. There was a twelve foot fence of close wire mesh. It appeared to be deserted. The car driver went around the camp through the gates – they were open, no sentry – and promptly stopped outside a low building with a corrugated roof. I noticed two other similar buildings. We all piled out, Eileen with her precious fur coat. She let me hold it once. I could only think how hot she must be with it always on her arm or lap, but no doubt it cost a lot of money and may not have been insured! She also wore some very large diamond rings and earrings. There was certainly a great deal of money on this lady. She was a very nice lady, quite down to earth and obviously both her husband and herself were self-made, moneyed people.

We went into the hut where the car had stopped. It was a long hut with a counter three-quarters along one side, with tables and chairs. On some tables there were condiments, rickety chairs and the tables covered in PVC tablecloths, very sticky due to the heat or maybe because they were not wiped regularly.

There were two pots bubbling on a dirty-topped hob. My husband leant over to have a look. It looked like some sort of stew. Very, very large chunks of meat in a dark grey glutenous mixture. The other looked similar, but was dark red and smelled of beetroot. I thought the meat was camel as there was no other animal I had seen that would measure up to such large lumps of meat. From a door, a man appeared suddenly. He pointed to the pots. My husband volunteered to try the stew and so did the two gay lads. I noticed some fruit, bananas and oranges, and all the ladies agreed. I was amused there was a chocolate slot machine on the wall. I could not believe chocolate would stay solid in that heat, plus there did not appear to be a slot for your money. The only drink available were bottles of Coca Cola. It was not ice cooled, but we were so thirsty, hot water would have been acceptable. Our driver had disappeared, not that he would have been much help, as whatever you asked, he continued to grin showing his brown teeth, plus I don't think he had washed for quite a while. Us ladies wanted to use the toilet facilities. When I look back, it was turning into a black comedy. After a mime, we were taken outside and were pointed to a hut that was hidden from the hut we had left. I was quite prepared for a hole in the ground and wondered how we would have any privacy, especially our nun traveller. The door opened outwards. Eileen went in first and we followed and to our amazement, a lovely tiled floor, three toilets and two wash basins and even a bidet! The only disconcerting thing was there were no doors on the toilets and no panes of glass in the windows which ran the full length of one wall. The toilets were like on a train, lever on the wall. I tried the taps. Nothing happened. They were not plumbed in, just ornamental. Over the years, sand had blown in and was around the base of the toilets, so if you sat down, your knees were almost level with your shoulders. Eileen quietly remarked it was like giving birth. The nun looked dismayed, our Dutch friend embarrassed, and I did not feel very comfortable either.

I had an idea and suggested we stood with our backs to the toilets whilst we took it in turns. As always, our Dutch friend gave me a hug and said, you are clever and of course we will be fine. The nun visually was relieved and thanked us profusely. My damp hand towel was passed around and although not refreshed, we came out feeling more comfortable than when we entered.

I later told my husband I found sand in places I did not know I had. As always, for the gents, they went behind a boulder and suchlike. I said they definitely did not deserve a star rating! I would complain to our travel agents. We stayed another twenty minutes and then the driver indicated we were leaving. We were only half way and more upset was yet to come.

The Dead Sea was impressive and so salty. I paddled. There were a couple of places to stay, I would not call hotels. We were keen to continue on our journey and after a further one and a half hours, we came upon a small town; one street, with buildings either side. People who were Arabs aimlessly seem to wander around and were curious at this motley of travellers. I think, but cannot remember accurately, this township was called Bathsheba!

Our driver had disappeared into one of the ramshackled buildings and promptly reappeared with a person who spoke broken English, telling us that he finished the journey in the car and we would be transported in another vehicle. He omitted to say what kind of transport. We soon found out. Eileen was sitting on her luggage on the road's edge and the lads had found two collapsible chairs and offered them to our Dutch friend and me. We took it in turns with the nun and Arthur, who was a rotund gentleman and was always wiping his brow and saying under his breath, I wish I was back in Cardiff High Street. He thought everything started and finished from Wales. He was very jolly and never showed any discontent. His humour was always evident and he would cheer you up. I learnt later that they owned three hotels in and around Swansea and the Mumbles. Their whole family were involved and that is how he could leave his hotels in their care and go travelling. They also had an apartment in Puerto Banús near Marbella. They had two sons and a daughter.

Down the road, or should I say track, to our amazement came on open-backed truck. It had a bench on each side and a cabin for the driver. It was quite high off the road and hard to get into. The driver spoke a little

English and beckoned to us to get in. He gave no assistance to the luggage and we had to load it ourselves. Needless to say, Eileen's took up the most room. The ladies sat down one side and the gentlemen down the other. Our legs were pinned under the benches because the luggage was piled up between us. Fortunately, our Dutch friend had a sunshade the size of a golf umbrella and it helped as it was hotter than ever. We were all beginning to feel drained and tempers frayed. Our nun took out her rosary and Arthur requested she said a prayer for each and every one of us.

The driver never seemed to know any other gear except second and we were all convinced Jerusalem would never be reached. Our Dutch lady always was upbeat and we started to sing 'Ten Green Bottles' and got up to twenty, before we gave in, as all throats were dry. What I would not have done for a cup of tea.

The journey took just over two hours and when we saw the outline of the Holy City, we all cheered and kissed each other. I'm sure the driver thought we were mad. As always, in adversity we were and had become good friends.

The two gay lads were in a different hotel to us and we never saw them again. Eileen and Arthur were staying at the 'King David Hotel' – very expensive. It was opposite our hotel which was called 'Shalom' – peace in Hebrew. Our Dutch friend was also staying and we met up every evening to talk on our events. Arthur and Eileen came over also. The nun was staying with colleagues at a retreat in the old city.

Jerusalem was a very interesting city and steeped in history. We visited the Wailing Wall. It was very strange, also very moving, with little notes left in the chinks in the wall and men rocking to and fro saying prayers. Above the wall was the Dome of the Rock, another religion and culture. We were allowed to go in, taking your shoes off. Totally different to the Jewish. Very quiet with magnificent carpets all around. The colours and decoration were breathtaking. The people worshipped very serenely and quietly. It was very impressive and when you thought how long it had been, amazing.

We visited Bethlehem, Nazareth, the Galilee, which I liked very much; quiet and brought back all the memories of what you knew in the Bible.

We took a train. It ran very slowly and you could smell orange blossom and pick fruit from the train. It was an open train, wood seats. Someone came along and you could buy cold drinks, oranges, bananas, and always barley sugar. The train took us to Jaffa. The city was very soft in colour – sepia, almost pink, when struck by the unrelenting sun. The skies were always blue and you realised you were in a totally different culture.

The only place we were not allowed off the coach was Hebron, where there were soldiers carrying guns. It was very busy and quite a big town. Our driver explained there was always trouble and it was in our interest not to be walking around.

I was disappointed in Bethlehem. There were TV aerials everywhere and it was very built up and no evidence of the fields where shepherds watched.

Nazareth had a beautiful church called The Annunciation – Christian. All along each side of the church were Madonnas from lands far and wide. From Great Britain, a silver Madonna. It was exquisite, full size. Japan's was a kimono, decorated in blue enamel and pearls. They were all beautiful and the lighting was in Mother of Pearl, shaped like tulips. It was like watching rainbows everywhere. I have never seen anything like it since. The wealth in that church must have been phenomenal.

As our holiday came to an end, we promised to keep in touch and we were going to ask for compensation for our journey through the Negev Desert.

We flew home from Tel Aviv, briefly as it was, it was good to feel the fresher air, being by the sea.

The following April we were invited to Eileen and Arthur's Ruby Wedding at one of their hotels and we in turn invited them as well as our Dutch friend to our Silver Wedding celebration in August. We kept in touch and visited until our situation changed, which I will relate later and explain. We did get compensation, which went towards our exciting holiday in the Far East in 1979.

1979 was a momentous year. Two holidays, our Silver Wedding date, a fire, losing half the roof on our house, a serious car accident, for me. For my husband, I feel on reflection the beginning of resentment and discontent started to fester. As I have said, he was not good at talking re. his feelings. Still very caring and loving towards me and our daughter, but business, no, he rarely discussed in depth.

I always knew when his annual tax accounts were due. Our lounge was covered in paperwork. He was always a super salesman, but did not enjoy the administration side of business. He always had good intentions, giving attention to everyday billing etc., but he would lapse and not be very disciplined. I offered to help on so many occasions, having done book-keeping at business college. He would thank me, but always declined, saying he knew what was going on and I had better things to do. After time, I did not persist as my help was always declined and I was sure he knew what he was doing.

In March 1979, we had a wonderful holiday in the Far East. This holiday was to mark twenty five years together, since the chance meeting in the cinema in late 1950.

We left Heathrow on a British Airways flight, stopping over at Rome and Dubai. My husband went walkabout in Dubai airport to stretch his legs, as it was the longest flight we had undertaken. We landed in Hong Kong. I was walking through the terminal, very jet lagged, tripped, and hit the tiled floor very hard and fractured my arm and wrist – we learned later in three places!

The service was amazing. Within fifteen minutes, I was in a private clinic, near the Peninsula Hotel, our hotel, being X-rayed, plastered and resting. I did not have a conventional plaster due to the type of fractures. My lower arm and wrist were on what looked like a wedge and stuck out to a right-angle, making it impossible nearly to wear my coat, dress, or whatever very easily. Eating with one valuable arm and going to the bathroom a real challenge. I was determined to enjoy this holiday. Four weeks away and as always, people are very caring and I had many supporters. My husband was very upset for me and said if I had to have an accident, why not on the last day, not the first. The clinic gave me excellent care plus all the paperwork and X-rays so when I returned home, my plaster could be removed in six weeks.

I had never been to such a busy place. You could have suits made in a day, silk shirts. You name it, it could be done. Although you never saw the work people, they are always on the go. So polite, nothing too much trouble.

We had arranged to meet some friends who lived on Hong Kong Island. We were invited for dinner and took the ferry from Kowloon to the island, where we were met by a Rolls Royce, maroon in colour, entering a circular drive to a type of colonial house – pillars and a long veranda, a light in every room, which was very welcoming. The owner of the house was the chairman of Imperial Tobacco.

Our host and hostess came to greet us. They were charming and very relaxed. The house was all white in decoration, except for a sweeping staircase and wrought iron balustrade in wood. The lady of the house collected 'frogs'. They were everywhere – in show cases, silver, Mother of Pearl, porcelain, ivory, doorstops, on the fireplaces and napkin rings on our dining table. The hall was very grand, with two large birdcages, painted white, housing coloured birds, and a white grand piano. The ceiling was domed and in pale green silk, pleated and beautiful tassels which when pulled concertinaed back to let the light in. The many sofas and chairs were also in silk, with cushions in pale green. It gave you a feeling of calm and I guess when very hot, coolness. We had a marvellous meal – lobster salad, followed by a ginger and almond ice-cream, wine and champagne, and iced coffee. A waiter helped me constantly with breaking up my food, so that I could eat with one good arm. My embarrassment was overcome as everyone was understanding and had sympathy for me. I thought I could get used to this. It was another dimension in my life. We were driven back to the ferry and invited to meet them and friends at a restaurant called The Pink Elephant – a circular building that slowly rotated, like the Post Office Tower in London. We had a great first week in Hong Kong and then flew onto Bali, Indonesia, for a further fourteen days.

Bali – on the not-too-long flight, we met three British people. A young man, about twenty five, called Chas. His name was Charles. Very entertaining, looked a little like Hugh Grant. Good mannered and very English. He was on a business/holiday trip for a company in London. A husband and wife from Croydon, who owned three garages. A holiday of a lifetime for them. They had never gone abroad before this time. All of us got on like a house on fire. Chas waited on me all the time. We had the same sense of humour. It was like joining a little club. We swapped ideas and experiences and we stayed all together for the rest of our holiday. A little like Israel, but different, as the culture and people were so different, so far away from home.

We were staying at the Bali Hotel – a hotel built around a compound of gardens and swimming pools. Very tropical and beautiful. Three restaurants, all with different cuisine; Western, Eastern and French.

One pool had a bar in the middle, where you could sip cocktails, keeping cool with your feet in the water, sitting on a high stool. Out of the question for me. I sat on the side and observed. The evenings were long and balmy and you only needed a cool dress, which wafted in the night breeze. All you could ever see, stars, clear skies, soft silver sand. Very romantic. Another world.

We usually all met up after lunch. We would sit under a bamboo hut. Waiters bringing drinks if you requested, going in the blue, blue sea, laughing, and generally just relaxing and talking about everything and anything. Our rainy green country a million miles away.

We went on two tours, into Jakarta – very dirty and busy. The people bathing alongside the roads, very polite and quiet in manner. I imagined water was very scarce and precious to the Balinese. The children were delightful. Big brown eyes and shy and I waved to them, with my good arm, all the time and always got a response. I think maybe curiosity, for my funny sticky-out arm. I used to have it wrapped in plastic, so I could go in the pool or sea. I did not want to miss out on the lovely warm water.

There were many Australians staying in Bali. Only a hop, skip and a jump for them to visit. They took the mickey out of me at every opportunity, call me the 'Pomme with the funny arm', amongst other things. It was always in good humour. I gave as good as I got. They could be very noisy, especially at drinking times. They would throw 'Fosters' into the pool and see how many they could drink! Not like the reserved 'Brits'.

After our fortnight was over, we flew to Singapore – the last part of our holiday.

Singapore was something else. So clean. Bins emptied, every hour on the hour. The women in dresses and the young men in trousers and white shirts, never jeans. Conventional haircuts and always polite, and excellent English spoken. We stayed at The Mandarin, Orchard Road. It was a very large hotel, the service excellent. In our large bedroom an orchid on the pillow, peppermints and bowls of fruit, and vases of orchids everywhere. Our bed linen was changed every day. Cleanliness impeccable. The food, Western or Chinese. The Chinese food totally different to our Chinese restaurants – much more monosodium glutamate in ours. For taste, I guess.

We went sightseeing of course. Raffles Hotel (I did see a cockroach there), Bugle Street, where transvestites appear out of the woodwork at 11:00 p.m. for sightseers and then disappear by 1:00 a.m. Never seen during the day. My better half bought me a lovely gold necklace. Always generous, too much for his own good sometimes. He was always the first to buy drinks and help anyone. A virtue I admired. My dad was the same. Sometimes taken advantage of and abused by takers in life, who get rich at your expense.

Although I liked very much being on holiday, three weeks is enough for me. I like coming home to familiar surroundings. The rain and always the green fields and sunshine always a bonus. I like seeing my loved ones and friends and my dog. Although it has not been tested, living abroad for a time would be fine, but I would always want to come home.

A friend of ours, who was a Battle of Britain pilot and later flew Lancaster bombers, always said when flying, he always sighed with relief when he saw the White Cliffs of Dover. He was home and felt secure and happy again. Later I will relate more adventures we had. The aforementioned gentleman and his wife and a fabulous holiday in Florence and Canada with them. Sadly, as I write, they are no longer in my life. Our last week in Singapore flew by and yet again, we promised to keep in touch with our newfound friends and invited them, if we had a party in August, our 25th wedding anniversary. Before relating that happy time, I will tell you about a 'big surprise' holiday taken only by me.

1979, May

A friend who had been widowed in August 1978, her late husband was an American, had died suddenly from a massive heart attack, aged forty five. He had asked his wife to visit the USA to celebrate his parents' Golden Wedding Anniversary in June 1979. She asked if she could come over and visit us. She lived in Ruislip. I said of course, come for supper the following evening.

She duly arrived and over our meal, she asked if I would consider accompanying her to the USA. It was going to be a very emotional journey for her and moral support would be very welcome.

I wanted to discuss with my husband, but my husband unhesitantly said, You must go. America is a great country. You will be made so welcome and there is so much to see. You won't believe you are on the same planet, it's so big! The idea was we would be away sixteen days, flying to Los Angeles, being met by our friend's sister-in-law, journeying to San Bernardino to stay a week with the parents of our American friend and decide when there our future plans. Maybe Anaheim, the oldest and first Disneyland, Orange County, through Los Angeles and then by coach down to Las Vegas, the Hoover Dam and onto the Grand Canyon, flying onto San Francisco for our last part of our visit. It sounded very exciting and hectic and as I had heard so many interesting things about the USA, I said I would love to go, albeit I was leaving my husband. He assured me it would be a good adventure and would be a chance in a lifetime. I think he was not keen to visit the USA in view of the outcome of his last visit, but as was his generous nature, would not stop me.

This was early May and we were travelling around the 20th. I cannot remember the actual date. I do remember we would be back in England early June. We were booked to fly on TWA, a direct flight. I did not notice jet lag this time.

My friend's relatives and in-laws met us at the airport. We travelled onto our dwelling for the next week – a very large mobile home with four bedrooms, large kitchen/dinette etc. The first thing I noticed about the USA, the roads through towns and cities were always flat, in blocks, with overhead traffic lights, doing the same speed, and I did not see any holdups, like here!

As we were guests and British, they pulled out all the stops with hospitality and mountains of food. All their friends came to visit and say welcome to their great country. I felt they were very patriotic to their flag and president, like we used to be, which I feel is a sad state of affairs and I hope may come back in time.

They took us out to dinner and again, mountains of food and salad bars continually replenished. To me, a side dish, to them, a meal in itself. I liked fresh water always available and little mats to hold your drinks on. I would have killed for a lamb chop. It was always steak. Surely the cows would run out with everyone eating beef. I also missed gravy and roast potatoes. Equally, I could get sick eating ice-cream for dessert at most meals. The weather was glorious and I guess your laundry would be dry as you were pegging it out. Whilst staying here, we visited Yosemite National Park. It was amazing. Waterfalls, mountains covered in beautiful trees right down to the base of the walkways and paths. The facilities and car parks excellent. People very friendly, especially when they heard you talk, always wanting to know where you lived in the UK and the royal family, weather and our history.

After the end of our stay, plans had been made to travel by coach to Las Vegas. We were staying at the Hacienda Hotel, all on one level. After booking in at reception, a buggy arrived and with our luggage, we travelled in the buggy for over a mile to our double room, overlooking a pool with Spanish influences, thus the name 'Hacienda'. It had over three hundred rooms, four restaurants, numerous gaming rooms which were active until 5:00 a.m., cleaned and then start again at 7:00 a.m. The service everywhere was first class and nothing was too much trouble. On our first evening, we had room service and then explored the layout and gambling rooms. We booked a late, late show – would have liked Sinatra or Sammy Davis, but had to make do with Eydie Gorme and Steve Lawrence, and Phyllis Diller. Again, the theatres adjoining the hotels were very big. You watched the shows with waiters always hovering to oblige with drinks, nuts, crisps, anything you wanted, within reason. All the establishments were very clean and no litter or tat. Always the staff, proud of their service and not frowned upon because they gave a service. The shows were like Hollywood musicals. Lovely dancing girls, orchestras, lasting on average two hours. There were three shows a night.

We stayed three nights and then continued by coach to see the Hoover Dam and after, the Grand Canyon. I had never seen a dam up close. It was overwhelming. A man-made miracle and hard to believe how millions of tons of water cascading down at the touch of a button. We did the usual tourist thing, photographs. It was very hot. We returned to our air-conditioned coach. It's too cold most of the time and she doesn't get an easy medium temperature. I seemed to take my jacket on and off on a regular basis. The coach had many different occupants – Japanese predominantly, German, two French, and we were the only Brits. The Japanese seemed to talk non-stop and always an octave higher than anyone else, and cameras everywhere and pork pie hats.

We were high up, but as the coach started to climb and the Grand Canyon came into sight, the first thing that came to my mind was the size. An enormous crater. I could not believe I was on the same planet. The Arizona River snaking silver along the canyon. I have never been good with heights – could not live in the mountains. I like seeing horizons. Later in my life I developed a very unpleasant disease, which included vertigo, spinning and nausea.

Back to the canyon. We were staying in a lodge, like a cabin. The hotel was in the middle and you walked down glass-covered walkways to the main building, which included two very large restaurants. You could sit outside, weather permitting. The restaurants were very spacious, with sofas, armchairs, a large bar, and tables and chairs when you ate. Once again I noticed the cleanliness and immaculate toilet facilities. Also, there were several canyon observation platforms. I found I could not go right up to the rail and always stood back and did not look down. My friend took the aeroplane and flew over the canyon. She said it was breathtaking and a little bit scary, as in places I believe the canyon is four miles deep. You can go down through a system of paths – that was not for me either. I felt on a cloudy day you could have touched the clouds. It is well-named, truly grand.

We stayed two nights/three days and then once again the coach took us to Phoenix and we flew to the last part of our adventure, San Francisco.

How I liked 'Frisco' very much; not so flat. Fisherman's Wharf, where we ate Lobster Thermidor. I have never had the same since – scrumptious.

The shops were large and as always air-conditioned and expensive. I did indulge and bought lovely percale bed linen, towels and accessories for the bathroom.

We flew home four days later. I wanted to see my husband again and of course my daughter and mother, who I had sent numerous cards to.

When we arrived at Heathrow, after all the kisses and hugs, my husband asked me to walk ahead with my friend's two daughters, as he had some sad news for our friend. While we were away, her father had died suddenly. The funeral had taken place. It was all pre-arranged by the British Legion at his request.

Needless to say, our friend was very upset, as we all were, and the excitement of the holiday in the USA was marred by this sad event. Equally, I have wonderful memories of my visit to the US of A. Later in 1982, I touched America again when I visited Canada and went to see Niagara Falls.

Now plans were being made for our Silver Wedding in August. More anticipation and excitement. I could not believe twenty five years had elapsed since that happy day.

We sent out forty eight invitations. My family, my mother, our daughter of course, two aunties, one cousin, my bridesmaid, and many friends from far and wide. The friends we had met on holidays. The venue was a hotel in Bagshot called Pennyhill Park. We had the party on the nearest Saturday to our anniversary, which fell on a Tuesday. It was going to be a dinner party with a small trio for music, who played very similar to the 'Carpenters'.

I bought a silver/blue chiffon dress, matched with a pair of strappy satin finish grey shoes.

It was a great evening. I had the wedding cake as promised by my husband, remembering the first one disaster. The only mar of the evening was a large mirror in the foyer fell off the wall and smashed everywhere, glasses on a table below and a lavish flower arrangement. I'm not superstitious, but what happened following this event could be seen to be an 'omen'.

Our friends, who we met in Israel, were staying the weekend, plus my mother. We had a good lunch on the Sunday, the conversation revolving around holidays, and they invited us to their 40th the following April. In the evening we took my mum to stay a few days with her friend Dorothy and our Welsh friends returned home on the Monday. Our actual anniversary was the following day. We had decided to go for dinner, just the two of us. We now had two poodles, Tweed and Jolie. Tweed was an apricot standard and Jolie a black miniature. Jolie I had adopted from a lady I had met and talked to at a literary lunch. The dog was her mother's who had recently died, leaving this little dog in a kennel in Epping Forest. She was unable to home him as she already had three Labradors. As soon as I heard he was a poodle, I said I would discuss this with my husband, but secretly I had decided I would home him and assured myself if he came down the path with his tail up, all would be well. He had been in the kennel twelve months and was obviously a survivor, as he was in a state – fleas, undernourished, and general lack of care. When we picked him up the following week, we went to a steakhouse, bought him a steak, cut it up and he gobbled it up and became one of the most loving and clever poodles, I was told. His kennel name was Scot. I changed it to Jolie and he lived up to his new name. Tweed really took to him and they were always great buddies. He lived the longest of all my dogs – eighteen – and was one of the cleverest.

We enjoyed as always our anniversary dinner and we both said how fortunate we both were to be so happy and to have found each other over twenty five years ago. Two days after our dinner together, things were back to normal. We went to bed and in the early hours of the night, we were aware the high wind was around our house and what seemed minutes, our roof was blown off and we were looking at a black sky. It seemed unreal and happened so quickly. The only noise, tiles hitting the patio and flying in every direction. I moved so quickly, as did my husband, downstairs, putting our dressing gowns on, getting hold of the dogs, who slept in the kitchen, out of the front door and stood in the road. We lived at the end of a cul-de-sac so no one was aware what had happened. Our house seemed to be the only one affected, as far as we could see!

We knocked on our neighbour's door. After a while they opened the door, taking time as they were asleep and had heard nothing, only aware of the high wind. They, without hesitation, asked us in and as always a cuppa of tea came. We could do nothing until morning and slept. Well, we didn't for hours, just tossed and turned, talking and wondering what would happen. Would we have to move out? Was it safe?

When daylight came, it showed three quarters of the roof had collapsed. You could see daylight in the three bedrooms. Pipes in the bathroom were exposed and the electrics not working. My husband telephoned his manageress to open the shop and gave a brief rundown on what had happened. He then rang our insurance, as all householders have to ask for advice. They were very helpful, gave us names and telephone numbers of companies re. roof tarpaulins, so that we could return home. They also said an assessor would come to view the damage and what we would have to do next. Our neighbours were marvellous.

In early 1979, I was once again approached about becoming a Justice of the Peace.

This time I did discuss with my husband and he told me to go for it. He said it would help me not to think so much about the absence of our daughter. I missed her so much and although she came to see us, usually for short visits, she never stayed over. Occasionally, we would go for a meal, but I felt we missed out on shopping, talking about boyfriends, always wondering if she was taking care of herself, eating sensibly and all the things mothers worry about for their children. I didn't feel needed anymore and it hurt. I asked many other mums – they said I was not alone. It didn't help or comfort me.

Back to being a magistrate. I went for a two hour interview before a panel of fourteen. I learnt afterwards, all magistrates. A week later, I received a letter saying yes and outlining training etc. It would take approximately one year. I had to attend as many courts as possible, just listen to procedure and cases tried. I had a book that was signed re. my attendances, how many hours etc. After nine months, I attended courses and seminars at a court in Reigate, with other candidates. We had to have a mock court and we took different roles – court officials, ushers, barristers, judge and so on and so forth.

It was very tiring, but I met some interesting people from different backgrounds and intelligence.

It was predominantly male and when I was sworn in at Kingston-on-Thames, there were three ladies and over sixty men new magistrates. Reams of reading matter came through the letterbox every week. I decided to take a speed reading course so I could absorb it all.

My husband attended my enrolment as a J.P. He said afterward, my voice did not falter during the swearing in, but he could see my hands shaking.

I had to sit on average twice a week in a court, usually eleven to twelve miles away, so if someone you knew came before the bench, you would have to 'sit back' for obvious reasons. If you could not attend, you had to ask another J.P. to sit for you. This arrangement worked well, as you would sit for them another date. I was nervous first time, but everyone was very helpful and the Clerk of the Court was always at your elbow to give advice and support.

Our husbands and wives were always invited to social events, Christmas parties, dinners and cocktail parties.

My husband and I had a private joke. I met so many J.P.'s called 'Muriel' for the ladies and 'Geoffrey' for the gentlemen. My husband would endure how many Muriels today and the same for the gents. Invariably, one lady sat/two gentlemen or two ladies and one gentleman would be the chair. Most were very friendly, others very stern and official.

The beginning of 1979 started well, but the end was very traumatic and unsettling.

After the roof incident, worse was yet to come!

September 19th, 1979

The date has always been imprinted on my mind.

We went to bed about 10:45 p.m. In my sleepiness I could hear the phone ringing. The instrument was on my side of the bed. I handed it to my husband, who was also awakened. After seconds he sat upright, was halfway out of bed and trying to find his trousers in the dark. I heard him say, Yes, yes, I'll come now. I had switched the light on and I said, Please tell me what is wrong. He was in such a hurry, but said it was the police – his shop was alight and it was going well. I too jumped out of bed and said I would come. He insisted I stay at home and he would telephone me as soon as he knew what was happening. He left within minutes and as his car drove away, I went downstairs, made some tea, and sat on the sofa. I really could not take it in and my mind was racing. How could this happen? Wiring? Surely not arson. So many thoughts.

I fell asleep on the sofa and was awakened once more. On looking at the clock, eight-ish. My husband, I could tell by his voice, distraught. The shop was burnt to the ground and the shops on either side were very much affected. The fire engines had left, the place was full of water, everything destroyed.

He was in the police station, as the first people they suspect is the tenant, for insurance purposes. I was also being asked to come to the station to be interviewed, for alibi purposes. I said of course I would come when I had showered and had some breakfast and join him. It was the first time in years, I knew my husband was close to tears.

When I arrived at the police station, I was ushered into a room, not seeing my husband first. I had to make a statement. I was interrogated for over an hour. Did I have any enemies? Was I involved with anyone else? Was I in bed with my husband when the telephone rang? Did we have money problems? It seemed never-ending and all the time I wanted to see my husband. I left the room after signing the statement and was reunited with my husband. We just clung to each other. No words were adequate to comfort each other. We left in separate cars and on the way home, passed the shop, which looked awful. It was too much and I wept all the way.

When something like this happens, your mind goes into overdrive. What happens next? The main thing being lack of funds. It could take months to be resolved. Insurance, assessors, builders – so many things to comprehend. One gets no support. You have to make phone calls, wait, wait and all the time, no income. My husband first rang his manageress, who was very upset and said, Try not to worry – I'll come back when you are back in business, and showed great loyalty. My husband said he would endeavour to pay her a holding salary until he knew what was happening. As usual, the insurance people were not perturbed re. time, re. rebuilding. I know it's their job, but no compassion was felt and always, we will be in touch and the usual expletives: don't worry. What a joke. Insurance companies are okay when you're paying your premiums, but never keen to pay up when what you are insured for comes into play. I do not have a lot of time or patience with the aforesaid.

It was given a short news bulletin on television the following evening, which I'm sure no one was particularly interested in.

A few days later, the fire service told us and the police it was arson. Petrol had been found in the store at the back of the premises and they were interviewing several suspects, who liked lighting fires! The shops on either side were also out of business. A café and a DIY. My husband and I went to see them. Needless to say, all of us were upset and felt we were in a wilderness.

We had savings, but when this happens, you just don't know what the future holds!

We both tried to be upbeat re. the situation, but I felt my husband lost a lot of enthusiasm re. business and maybe life in general. On looking back, I feel sure so.

The insurers chose a builder across London and to our dismay, they did not start work until 10:00 a.m. and finished at 4:00 p.m. As we were going into the darker evenings and always as seems the norm then and today, tea brew-ups were frequent and talking and progress was very slow. We asked for a time schedule and they vaguely said early May 1980 – exactly eight months. My husband was very troubled. No income and losing the goodwill of the business. The public understandably move on to fresher fields and soon forget. You have to win that all back and it's very hard.

Christmas was not a cheery one and my husband hated doing nothing. He had always been a workaholic and you can only do a certain amount of jobs around the house. He would be very short-tempered and nothing you could say or do made the situation any easier. Our savings soon dwindled and that added fuel to the fire, excuse the pun!

My forty seventh birthday came and went and as usual my mother was with us. She had been very supportive and not so demanding during this time and of course we had no reason not to visit – both of us.

I decided besides my J.P. work, I would find a job. I very quickly got an office part-time job in a dry cleaners in Sunningdale.

Very small staff, good lady employer. I worked three hours every afternoon and Saturday mornings on my own. I often wished so much my dad was around, as my husband and he communicated so well and I felt it would have made the situation easier to bear. My dad was always optimistic and my husband being born under the scales, 'Libra', up and down and when he was down, very low.

Four months after this event, the police informed us a suspect had been arrested for arson. He had set two other fires in the county.

We attended the court hearing to hear his fate! He had a custodial sentence of two years! Two years for ruining three people's livelihood, giving financial problems and in some cases, never recover in business terms. Although a person involved in the law, I felt there was very little justice for the victims. He would be out in one year, to do more deeds no doubt, as they have no monitoring or supervision to find out why they light fires.

More upset. I was travelling to my part-time job which I really liked. It was about 1:45 p.m., travelling on a fairly straight B road, doing approximately thirty miles per hour. Without any warning a Land Rover with a high horsebox being towed came out of a concealed entrance, took the turn too acutely and the box tipped over onto the bonnet of my car. The horse fell out on its back across the bonnet, making the car settle, and I was pinned by my legs in the car. The roof of the car also caved in and I could not move.

The horse owner went into panic. I learnt later he was going to Smith's Lawn to play polo and was late. The poor horse was flailing about, terrified, as I was. I was afraid the car would catch fire and I would not be able to move.

Fortunately, a motorist proceeding the other way had seen a police car near an oncoming roundabout and immediately turned around to alert them. What seemed ages, a fire engine and ambulance were there. I had to be cut out of the car, which took ages. The medics were efficient, talking to me through the window and one crawled in through the rear window and gave me an injection for pain. All this time the horse was crying out in pain and to my horror had to be destroyed.

I was taken to the local hospital with a fractured tibia and a broken ankle on my other leg, and in deep shock.

I woke up in hospital, my husband holding my hand, with more worry lines than before, saying, "Oh how glad I am you're safe. Don't worry about the accident".

All I could say was, "It comes in threes – the roof, the fire, and now this incident," and he replied, "I certainly hope so!"

I made him smile by saying, "When I fill out the insurance details, it will be different – a horse falling on my car. Maybe a first".

The driver of the Land Rover came to see me, full of apologies. Said he had been reckless because he was late for the polo match.

In late May 1980 our shop was back in business, thank goodness. It was good to see my husband enjoying refurbishing the interior. Stock had to be bought and displayed. It was a great relief to us both. I did think my husband did not have the enthusiastic spark, but it was understandable. It had been a great setback and very expensive. What was good was the shop had good passing human traffic, being near the station and a Post Office opposite, but it took time and patience to build up clientele again. I knew it would not take too long, as my husband was a very good front man and selling came like second nature.

I recovered from the accident, did my Bench work and decided to continue my part-time job, which I really enjoyed – meeting the public on a day-to-day basis, many celebrities lived in and around Sunningdale/Ascot and they came into the office. Bruce Forsyth, Bernard Gallacher, The Tremeloes, Kenny Lynch, Jimmy Tarbuck, Diana Dors. We were on first name terms. It was and did remind me of my happy time in Baker Street.

Our re-entry into business had a blip when several months after opening, the arsonist who had been prosecuted came into the shop and bragged about his offence, saying, I lit your shop, good eh! I was furious to think, what good punishment. He no doubt would re-offend and upset other people's lives – is this justice?

You will see by the end of my narrative, justice runs like a river through my writing, or lack of it!

1981

We went into the New Year, me another year older, my husband back in business, our daughter really enjoying her job, sharing a house with a friend in Reading.

As always, my mum spent Christmas with us and did hint re. moving. I did not make any pressure, but it raised my hopes. I was always juggling my Bench work, part-time job and driving to see her.

We went to Spain with our friends for the sixth time. We got on so well, always rented a villa with a pool. This time it was Estepona on the Costa del Sol. We spent an idyllic time, bathing, sun and good food. We found two restaurants which were first class – Swedish and Spanish – family-run restaurants.

We also spent a lovely day in a sumptuous villa in the mountains overlooking Marbella. Some friends who I had met working as a J.P. had moved out there permanently. We also went to Granada, which was an experience, which I will relate.

My husband spoke quite decent Spanish, so we left all the travel details to him. We had hired a car, drove to Malaga Station, caught the train to Granada, having to change midway. We left at 9:45 a.m. The train facilities left a lot to be desired – wooden seats and no toilet facilities. At the midway stop, we had to cross over a bridge to another platform. All went well, until our female friend was violently sick. She tried to find, well all of us did, a facility on the platform we had just alighted from. She told us to carry on and when she had composed herself, would follow.

I guess you will realise what happened. We were boarding the train and it left without her. We were hanging out of windows as she was running along the platform, saying we will wait at Granada for the next train.

She duly arrived one and a half hours later. We, of course, were sitting waiting for her.

We arrived at the hotel my husband had booked previously. Two maiden ladies, sisters I think, they spoke excellent English. We went to our rooms. It was very hot and decided to have a rest and meet down in the reception at 6:00 p.m.

Now my husband had booked the Parador for our evening meal. It was his birthday and we were going to push the boat out. Our friend had recovered and we laughed re. the incident at the station.

Both my friend and I had cool dresses on and the boys looked good too. We went out into the street, hailed a taxi – our friends sat in the rear and my husband alongside the driver. He spoke to the driver in Spanish: Parador, por favour. (I hope that's correct.) The driver replied, Si. We all understood that. The taxi did not move. After three more attempts and the same reply, Si, he pointed across the road. There was the Parador, right opposite our hotel. We piled out of the rear of the car, falling about laughing. My husband never lived it down. Whenever we were going anywhere, we would say, Leave it to you and start laughing all over again. The taxi driver murmured 'stupid English'. We did not care. Our sense of humour came to our aid in a silly situation.

We had a sumptuous meal and it was a memory that would not be forgotten.

We stayed another whole day in Granada and went to see the Alhambra which was fascinating. The architecture and water fountains everywhere, beautiful tiles and moorish influences. Well worth a visit.

We returned the next day, this time by coach. It was much more comfortable, took longer and it was so hot. We picked up the car again and motored back to Estepona and our villa.

We spent many happy times together as a foursome and went eight times to Spain, before it got so commercial, as I believe it is now, and so much building of holiday homes and Brits retiring in the sun.

In early May 1981, my mum had a stroke.

The hospital admitted her for observation and tests. The consultant was optimistic, as she did not lose her speech or use of her limbs. Her memory was impaired and all things considered, she was recovering. After ten days she was allowed home and without question, I insisted with me, as she was nervous of being on her own in the bungalow. I told her she could stay as long as she liked. Over the following months, we discussed many times that she moved nearer and even an annex was mentioned, as we had plenty of room, for one to be built on the side of our home. Although I felt we were making progress, it was her decision. She returned to the bungalow in late July.

On one of my weekly day visits, over lunch, Mamma said I do not want to spend another winter here, so can we look for a ground floor flat or maisonette. I was over the moon about this decision. I suggested she put the bungalow on the market and in turn, when I returned home, I would put her name and requirements on estate agents near where we lived. My husband too was pleased a decision had been made, not only for Mamma, but myself, as six years commuting to visit was stressful.

On my return I put the wheels in action and within forty eight hours, details were coming through the post. Mamma had two viewings for her home and within a few days, it was sold, subject to contract. The couple were retiring, like my parents, and were moving out of London for a quieter life. I hoped they had more years in retirement than my parents. They were renting and wanted to be in occupation by late September/early October.

Some details came through the post which I felt would suit Mamma very well. It was a maisonette a mile from our home, two years old. The lady resident was going in a residential home.

I went down to bring Mamma back for a view. It was first class. Large lounge with viewing to the front, with passing traffic and people; something my mother had missed when she moved. One double bedroom and a smaller one, which could have been suitable for a small dining room. A galley kitchen, bathroom and separate toilet. A handkerchief front and back garden, double glazed. It was very well-appointed. A lady lived upstairs – she was still at work, so it would be quiet. It was near the shops and a large Waitrose. It would take me ten minutes from my home to visit every day.

Mamma was a cash buyer, so there would be no problems there. She showed great enthusiasm and I promised once again, if and when anything happened, I would take her to be buried with my dad.

Our friends had invited us for a holiday in their holiday home in West Wittering, Sussex. We could take the dogs. I may have said before, my husband had bought me a standard apricot champagne poodle. I called her 'Tweed' and her companion was Jolie, a black miniature. They looked like little and large. She was a lovely-natured poodle and once again I had struck gold. She was a great conversation-maker as whenever I took her out, people would stop and admire. We agreed and thanked our friends and decided to stay ten days. We took our own car, as they spent a great deal of time there in good weather during the summer. We celebrated my husband's birthday again and on the last Friday of our stay, I suggested we motored down the coast to visit Mamma. She had been very enterprising and had a garage sale. My suggestion, something very popular in the USA. I was so pleased for her, as she had not been sentimental and got rid of articles she had not used for five years. I advertised the sale in local shops and on the morning there was a patient queue waiting in anticipation and she sold everything.

We decided to go unannounced. I was glad I did. I let myself in the side door – it was always unlocked. I also had a key of course. The kitchen looked unusually untidy – ginger ale bottles on the worktop, the blind down. I called out 'Mamma' and walked into the lounge. Mamma was sitting on the sofa, in her dressing gown. Very unusual. Throughout her life, even when she was very unwell, she always got dressed.

I sat down beside her and said, "What's wrong?"

She was very flushed and wheezy on her chest. She said, "I have a tummy upset and dreadful indigestion. I have been drinking ginger ale to try and alleviate it. I do feel better than this morning."

"Don't worry." I said I would call the doctor.

She protested and said, "It will pass. I've seen enough of doctors in my life. I've got a hot water bottle and tea for comfort," and she kept reassuring me that she would be fine. "Nothing can happen now, I'm moving in two weeks and I'll see you every day, won't I?"

We stayed three hours. She insisted we return to our friends and I promised to telephone the next morning, Saturday, also saying she could return with us. It would be easy to pick her up on our way home from West Wittering.

I telephoned at approximately nine-ish. There was no answer. I thought good, Mamma is feeling better and has gone shopping. As a second thought, I also rang her neighbour and asked if he would kindly go around to see if all was well. I held on and within a few moments, he returned and said he looked through the bedroom window and saw Mamma on the floor. I told him to call an ambulance immediately and I would ring back. I told my husband and friends and once we knew what hospital, would leave and motor to the hospital. What seemed like ages, I rang again and her neighbour had let the ambulance people in and Mamma was going to Southampton General Hospital.

It took us about half an hour to reach the hospital, contending with Saturday traffic. I ran into reception whilst my husband parked the car. I was directed to a ward on the second floor. I went into the ward. A sister was sitting at her desk in the middle of the ward. You always knew nurses. Their lovely starched caps and silver belt buckle. Not like today, you don't know who is who. I could not see Mamma. I asked and she said tests and X-rays were taking place and Mamma would return within the hour. So she beckoned me to an empty bed and said relax, she will be back soon, don't worry.

Mamma waved and smiled on her return to the ward. Apologising for bringing us there and saying she did feel easier and her indigestion had subsided. We stayed all day, except for lunch downstairs in the canteen. At about six-ish, I asked if I could stay the night and they immediately agreed and said I could have a room on a ward one floor below. My husband left at about 7:30 p.m. and we agreed if all went well, he would motor down when I was ready and we knew the outcome of tests and Mamma's stay in hospital.

The sister said she would let me know re. any developments, but to bear in mind Mamma was seventy nine and her general health was poor, due to years of asthma and other chest complications.

Mamma and I chatted re. her move in a fortnight's time and how much she was looking forward and me seeing her every day.

Lights went out in the ward at about 9:00 p.m. and I went to my room. The nursing staff were kindness personified and without asking brought tea and biscuits and said they would awaken me in an instant, if need be.

I kissed Mamma and told her I was only downstairs and would see her tomorrow.

About 11:40 p.m. I was awakened by a nurse, who said, I think you should come. We ran along the corridors as quietly as possible.

All the lights were off in the ward, except the curtains and light over my mother's bed. Mamma was sitting up looking very hot and uncomfortable. I held her hand and she was lucid and said what a good daughter and how proud Daddy and I were of you always. She said she was very tired and wanted to go home. She closed her eyes and slipped away, forever and always. I was devastated. There had been no indication, at least to me, that she was going to die.

After ten minutes, the kind nurse took me into another room, brought me some tea, said how sorry they all were. My mother had severe renal failure and pulmonary oedema, her heart was weak due to years of asthma etc.

I went back to my room and could only think that at least she would get her wish and be with my dad.

I did not telephone my husband. It was just past midnight. The nurse asked me if I would like a sleeping pill. I refused and after what seemed ages, fell asleep.

I was woken up by hospital nurses and got dressed, went to see Sister to ask what I should do. She said Mamma's death certificate would be ready on Monday. It was now Sunday. I asked if I could telephone my husband. He was very upset and wished he could have been with me, but said she did not die alone, like a large percentage of people do. I asked him to ring Mamma's two sisters. One I knew would be very kind and understanding, and the other (her eldest sister) was cross with me that I had not told them Mamma was ill. My only explanation, being it had all happened so quickly and I had no idea of the outcome.

My husband said he would travel down and pick me up from the hospital. We would go back to the bungalow and inform our daughter and friends, wait until Monday to get in touch with the undertaker etc. It was October 1st.

As expected, Mamma's eldest sister did not show compassion and told me off for not telling her Mamma was unwell. I explained how quick events had happened. As usual she was not particularly interested in my explanation, just said to let her know arrangements and she would endeavour to attend.

My other auntie (from Gibraltar) was kind and very upset and said she would telephone me again to hear re. funeral arrangements.

Mamma was cremated, by her request, on October 8th, my dad's birthday. At a later date I scattered her ashes, near his on a hilltop near their home.

Mamma's solicitor telephoned his condolences and assured me re. the sale of the bungalow and would inform the estate agents and solicitor re. the maisonette Mamma was going to purchase. I felt it had all happened too late, but life deals these blows and decisions come too late.

The following weeks were hectic. I had to see Mamma's solicitor, the transfer of name on the bungalow deeds so the sale could still go through. Mamma had been wise and left a will. She instructed I give away all her effects to either our daughter or myself, the rest of the family and friends. My aunt was there, asking what I was going to do with this and that, dinner service (although she had two already), carpet and several ornaments. My aunt since being widowed at thirty six had never had to work. Her late husband came from a wealthy family, builders. She lived in the house her husband had built and was very comfortable. She would scan the newspapers for bargains and would travel across the town she lived in for a bargain and at one time had four vacuum cleaners and many other items. She was very covetous and never generous with her family.

I said if she would like to travel up to my parents' bungalow, I would meet her there and take it from there. She agreed and on the day left with my mother's medical mattress on the top of the car, the bedroom carpet and the dinner service and would have taken a great deal more if I had not intervened. When I visited her home months later, it was like going to my mother's home. She never wrote or thanked me, just believed because she was the eldest sister – her right.

The people who were buying the bungalow were quite prepared to wait longer for probate and moved in a month later than planned. On the day before completion, I went to the bungalow for the last time. I felt very sad and lonely. Both my parents had gone and no one to talk to about my young days and happy events. The only time I would have liked a sibling to relate to. I left some flowers and good wishes to the new occupants and told them to be guarded re. the neighbours and their noisiness.

The other great occasion that happened in 1981 was the royal wedding – the Prince of Wales and Lady Diana Spencer – in July. Again, ending so unhappily and disastrously with the Princess being killed in a car incident in Paris.

All these events overshadowed our daughter's 21st birthday in August. As always she did not want a 'bit of a do' and we went out to dinner with her present boyfriend to make four of us. Her choice of cuisine and we gave her two Georg Jensen bracelets which she always wears.

1981/2 Christmas seemed odd without my mother's presence. I decided to remember both my parents with a memorial plaque in the churchyard in the village we lived in. On a Remembrance Wall, I planted a Golden Showers rose, my dad's favourite.

1982

As I have said before, my birthday is at the very beginning of each year. This year it fell on a Sunday and I was nearly 50, in 1983.

My husband said he had booked lunch in the VIP restaurant in Heathrow. It was mainly because I loved watching aeroplanes taking off and landing. It was a low cloud ceiling and misty but dry day. We left at approximately 10:30 a.m. It took about thirty five minutes to Heathrow. As always the place was buzzing. We sat down and ordered coffee, as lunch was booked for twelve noon.

There is always something going on at airports and could happily spend a day just watching the people, wondering where they were going and coming from.

I was aware that the tannoy was, I thought, calling my name. I looked at my husband who was smiling and, That's for you! I did not know what to think. Why me, being paged now to go to the reception desk? I did just that and I was given an envelope with my Christian name on it. Opened and there was a ticket to fly on 'Concorde'. I was speechless. I always would run out in the garden and watch it become airborne and admire the grace of this beautiful aeroplane. I ran back to my husband and said we are flying on Concorde. He assured me I was, but he was not and would be waiting for me. I was leaving now, having lunch on the aeroplane, flying around the Bay of Biscay, going through Mach 1, 2 and 3, and of course having this wonderful experience. Evidently my husband had joined the Concorde Club and if you were a member, had the opportunity to fly with other members.

I reluctantly said au revoir to my husband, went through the gate and entered this magical aeroplane.

The first impression was how small the interior was. Two seats either side of a middle aisle, sumptuous leather seats, leg room, nearly an armchair.

We were welcomed by the captain and all the crew. He shook hands with everyone and wished us a happy time on Concorde.

My feet were only just touching the ground. I wanted to take everything in as I knew this was a once-in-a-lifetime experience and my birthday!

The pilot made the journey very interesting, telling us when we went through Mach 1 and 2 and seeing the arc of the earth below.

It all went too quickly and we were back in Heathrow. My husband, through the staff on Concorde, gave a gold Concorde charm for my bracelet, a silk scarf of Concorde flying through the clouds and the hostess gave me a Concorde glass when they sang Happy Birthday. We arrived around 4:00 p.m. My husband was waiting and the journey home was all the experience combined with kisses and thanks for a marvellous experience, never to be forgotten.

When Concorde flew for the last time, I went to say farewell as she flew over the Bristol Suspension Bridge to fly into Filton.

The rest of the year was uneventful. We had our usual holiday in Spain with our friends.

September, 1982
Our visit to Canada.

Our next door neighbours, who now lived in Maidenhead, asked us if we would like to visit Canada. We also had close friends who lived there. They were Canadian born and met in the forces just prior to 1939, in England, married, and after the war came back to the UK and only decided to retire back to Canada in 1980. They lived in Kelowna B.C. and were always asking us to visit. We had already had our Spanish holiday, but decided it would be good.

The friends we were going with was the Battle of Britain pilot and his wife I have spoken of previously in this manuscript. He was hoping to meet up with his navigator in Lancaster Bombers who had after the war emigrated to Canada. All of us had a purpose for the visit.

Our itinerary was Vancouver, Kelowna, Banff, Calgary and Montreal. We would be away a month from September to early October.

We left Heathrow on a BA flight direct to Vancouver. We arrived late at night and booked into our pre-booked hotel. We were staying four days, leaving on the 5th to our friends in Kelowna.

Vancouver is a lovely city – clean and it all looked spanking new, especially the buildings. Gastown had a lot of English features. Restaurants were abundant and next to San Francisco the largest community of Chinese, and their restaurants were very evident, as well as excellent food. Canadians were very friendly, especially as they originated from the old country and many referred to it as the home country.

On the first morning, I went down to reception and the young lady immediately said, "Isn't it terrible about the princess?" I thought she was referring to our Royals, but it was Princess Grace of Monaco who had been killed in a car in France.

Our visit to Vancouver was a great introduction to Canada and we went to Prince Edward Island and also Vancouver Island, again with many English influences. We visited two large parks, the fall was just beginning and the trees spectacular.

We travelled by coach to Kelowna, our journey taking from 8:30 a.m. to 6:00 p.m. Again, the countryside was lovely. Our friends met us and we travelled fifteen minutes out of the town to their bungalow overlooking a large lake. The scenery had changed, as we were at the beginning of the Rockies.

Our friends were very hospitable. We had our own suite in the basement, a lounge, bathroom, toilet facilities, and our other friends their own bedroom and lounge. We all met up after resting for 'happy hour' in our friends' lounge and dinner followed at 7:30 p.m. Happy Hour was a ritual when we would all relate our news of the day. Our friends had even laid on a car, so we could do our own events.

Kelowna was a very attractive town. Again, cleanliness was very evident, and a great deal of the shops and facilities revolved around the lake, a little like lakes in Switzerland. Houses hugging the shoreline, a large mall in the centre of town. Also the bus travel was very good and many retired population lived there, like our Bournemouth to London.

Our friends were very good hosts. We laughed a lot, reminisced and nostalgia took over sometimes, but our visit was memorable and when I, alone, visited in 1992, it was just the same, except our host was in bad health and in a home. Our hostess had moved into a condominium. I spent Christmas in Canada with my friend. She had sent me a return ticket as a Christmas gift – very generous – and at a time when I really needed companionship and to recharge my batteries.

We once again left Kelowna reluctantly, to travel further into the Rockies to the resort of Banff. We visited a real old castle-type hotel. The cast of Doctor Zhivago was filmed there. There was certainly a lot of snow. Walking was easy as the walkways were always clean and safe underfoot.

Banff was one long road with hotels on the perimeter, mainly a town for tourists, and your first glance of the magnificent Rockies. It was also a ski resort and very busy in the winter months. We spent a week there seeing as much as we could. Our holiday friends were very good company. We got on famously and they would decide re. eating one evening and we the next. David's (now deceased) navigator friend was at our next stop – Calgary.

We flew to Calgary across the prairie – it took about two and a half hours. We arrived around 5:00 p.m. Our friends were staying with their friends and we stayed in a hotel nearby. Our stay was for only two days.

Of course, Calgary is the famous Rodeo City – very flat and I found uninteresting. A big business centre.

We met up at the airport and continued onto Montreal where we were staying the longest, taking in Niagara and surrounding towns. We stayed in a Ramada Hotel – very big and very busy. We went to a baseball match and did a lot of sightseeing and shopping. I always try and bring a memento that is traditionally of the country and this time. I have three copper maple leaves that are in my lobby, reminding me of the beautiful fall we were experiencing and Canada on the whole.

For me, Niagara was outstanding. We went by coach and you could hear the water two miles before it came into sight. The village called Niagara was where we stopped for coffee. Very picturesque and charming. Every house looked manicured and unreal. I felt it would have been a good backdrop for 'Stepford Wives'.

Although I do not like heights, I managed to go up close to the falls and we took the boat underneath that is put on for tourists. You can't have a good hair day at Niagara as there is a constant mist in the air. We of course seeing it from the Canadian side, but I guess wherever you were it would be an awesome sight.

Montreal has some lovely parks. We visited them all and always made very welcome, and a great deal of Scots from the old country that had settled there.

Reluctantly, we left Canada for our return home, receiving a great welcome from our standard poodle 'Tweed' and 'Jolie' our miniature.

A memorable holiday and many good memories with our friends – sadly no longer here.

Our daughter was living in a top floor flat near Clapham Common. She had a regular boyfriend who she had known since her teenage years. Her hairdressing was very vibrant and she was always busy. She came to see me regularly, but I often wished she would stay over so we had more time together. I still missed her very much. I took on more J.P. work, joining different panels – Juvenile Court and Licensing. It helped filling the gap of not having to visit my mother. Probate had gone through without any problems. I talked to my husband and I decided to pay off our mortgage. Always to everyone something that is in twenty five years of life, whatever happens.

In 1983, my 50th birthday was celebrated with a dinner party of twelve of our friends. Little did I know this year would bring changes, quite dramatic and worrying.

My husband announced out of the blue, he was selling his business. I was taken aback, as he seemed content and business was fine, and although he often said it was not the same after the fire, business seemed back to normal. As I have said before, my husband never talked to me re. money. I was always interested and would have helped in any way. I don't know whether it was pride and confrontation was not on his agenda. I had always trusted him and put it on one side. He said he was going to try property development – buying houses and converting them into flats etc. He had no experience of this, especially finance-wise. He was a good DIY person, but not I felt on this level. He assured me he knew what he was doing, but I did have concerns.

I often wished my dad was around. He was always a good listener and wise in counsel.

He sold his shop very quickly and by October 1984, he bought a Victorian house in Battersea. The conversion was straightforward after getting planning permission. It was in quite good order. The accommodation was two one-bedroom flats with separate entrances, new bathrooms and kitchens, decorating, plumbing and electrics. He did say he thought the ground floor would be ideal for our daughter, as an investment, and the top floor ideal for a business person.

He left the house every morning at 7:00 a.m. The journey took just over an hour. He worked very hard, took evening classes to learn plumbing, but subcontracted the electrics, rewiring etc.

He took a large bank loan to fund the project and hoped to sell at a profit to buy the next house. Redevelopment at this time was very popular, but financially precarious as like it has always been, greedy re. banks and their pound of flesh.

On the home front we did not have a regular income and I felt my husband was a little out of his depth as the time turnover can be very precarious. He had always succeeded in all his endeavours and I hoped and prayed this project would be safe, for his sake. The fire incident had been a dreadful setback in his life and dented his confidence.

We talked to our daughter re. the idea of her having the ground floor flat, as her present situation was not good. Paying a landlord rent indefinitely gets you nowhere and her facilities were not 100%. The bathroom facilities on another floor below and the smallest kitchen I had ever seen, very claustrophobic and cold, being an attic flat. All went well re. this idea.

The second house conversion was not so good.

He bought another house for conversion. Two-point-two beds this time. All went well until it came to selling. The bank was charging large interest rates, and living off the proceeds of his shop sale, it soon dwindled away. He was very despondent and although he never admitted it, realised we could not make a living in this way. The last conversion took eight months to sell. The bank would not continue with loans and our situation was in trouble.

Creeping into conversation was he thought he may have to go back into having another business. Something he knew. Having a shop. I'm sure this failure really knocked his pride and again I felt discontent was now in his character. Outwardly, you would not have known anything was wrong. We still went out to dinner, socialised, and when I queried the expense, he told me not to worry, he knew what he was doing. I noticed he was buying Daltons Weekly for businesses. He dearly wanted another business in the area so we did not have to move. We both loved our present home. Indeed, it was my favourite home. We had been there since 1967 and had many friends and we were well-established. It was not to be. Everything was very expensive and we lived in an expensive area. My husband showed me a write-up on a Post Office plus adjoining shop on the Isle of Wight.

My heart fell, but I hoped he would consider all the options and make a good decision.

Over a weekend we went by car to Portsmouth and took the ferry across to Ryde.

He had made an appointment to view the premises. The Post Office making an added income that was paid separately from the shop business. The location was outside Ryde, about six miles. A through village with just the Post Office etc. being the main trading.

I had been to the island for a short holiday and it was delightful, but like many locations, living all year round is entirely different.

I was not very impressed with the present ownership. They were not very friendly and made no effort to sell the business. There was a first floor flat adjoining the main shop, a long and unkempt garden, garage adjoining. The flat had two double bedrooms, large dining room and lounge overlooking the road, a galley kitchen, and separate toilet and bathroom. The building formerly had been a bakery; the shop having been the bakery and the adjoining buildings, the living accommodation. On our return home, he said if we decide, we would stay five years and return to the mainland and retire.

We waited another month. Nothing came our way and in desperation we decided to move to the island. This happened in September. My husband had to be interviewed by the Royal Mail to run the Post Office and of course the solicitors took their time and our money to buy the business.

One good thing, it was a freehold business and when sold we had no overheads like rent and lease to find. We were very underfunded and yet again had to have a large mortgage. I could not believe in five years we could retire and worried re. my husband's aspirations. I once again wished he had been more forthcoming. I often asked. He always told me I worried unnecessarily and why did I question his decisions. He just would not discuss my concerns and after a while I gave up, as it only caused discord. You can't change people and in all other aspects he was a caring man.

We were unable to move until late November. We sold our house for cash and after paying the flat's outgoings, conversions etc., had just about enough to pay a 10% deposit on our new mortgage. Sadly, we left our Surrey home in early October and rented a cottage in Cornwall, waiting out until we could move to the island. All our friends and our daughter were surprised at this move and yet again I felt my husband's pride was severely dented.

About this time my favourite cousin, who had shared our first home with his wife Jo, was diagnosed with stomach cancer. He was just forty nine. A terrible blow. My auntie had lost her husband in 1975, like my dad. My auntie went to live nearby their home to be near during his illness. It was a very distressing time for everyone and I visited as often as I could.

The move was very traumatic. It cost over £1,000 to move our furniture across the water. It was done over three days. It poured with rain and the English Channel was uninviting, grey skies and gave us no cheer.

Our first introduction to the islanders was glum. They referred to us as mainlanders and they certainly gave no welcome to the owners of their Post

Office. I was full of foreboding. I had hoped to do my court work, made all enquiries, but they had a full register of J.P.s and gave no inclination any vacancy would occur. My husband gave into my pleas and let me work part-time in the shop. The other hours being taken by the staff we inherited.

Our first Christmas on the island was very quiet and time for us to take stock. Two people knocked on our door on Christmas Day asking for produce, something we had not encountered before and because we lived over the business, my husband hated this, as he felt entitled to one day off in three hundred and sixty five.

Into the new year 1984, nothing changed. The islanders were very close and there was no sociability. We both missed our daughter and friends. Life I felt took a downfall. My light at the end of the tunnel was accepting we would hopefully be on the mainland in five years. Life became routine – the shop, Post Office business. My husband found the confinement of the Post Office very claustrophobic and monotonous. Good job we loved each other and liked each other's company. There was nothing else. It wasn't the island, just the people on it. I cannot recall any good times except when our daughter and her boyfriend visited, and our friends.

In December, my cousin died. His funeral was in North Harrow, the church where they worshipped. It was a very sad day and next to the demise of my parents, another person who had figured so much in my young life. Someone who had always been caring, through the war and after. Not only did I feel for Jo, his wife, but my auntie, losing her only son so young.

In early June, a Royal Mail official came into the shop, was talking to my husband at length. He left and my husband came through the shop, put closed on the door, took my hand and we went up to the flat and dropped a bombshell!

The Royal Mail were closing the Post Office, along with three others on the island. A new Tesco supermarket was being built and the Post Office would be nearby. More customers, more money.

It was the first time my husband wept openly and kept saying what can we do? Without the Post Office we would lose all the goodwill and trade and the shop alone would not sustain our living there. We did not go to bed that night, just talked about our options. We decided we had no option but to leave the island.

My husband never went down to the Post Office again.

The Royal Mail had given us six weeks before it closed. He said if they gave him no consideration, neither would he.

The very next day, we got in touch with estate agents and asked them to come and see us. My husband put a notice on the door, 'closed until further notice' and to contact the Royal Mail for enquiries.

The estate agents were full of woe. We had bought the business for £93,000 and they said it was likely we would not be able to raise £40,000, if we were lucky. They suggested we tried to sell it with planning permission for living accommodation, converting the shop into a dwelling, as there was no value in the shop without the Post Office.

We were both so very disappointed that what we had hoped was a second chance, we had nothing. My husband was fifty three years old. The time when your mortgage payments were nearly over and looking toward winding down with retirement no too far away.

It was a bitter blow. On reflection, I feel events festered from this time and I felt my husband would find it hard to recover. He also thought about his image and what our friends would think of the mess we were in. No one came to view at all and after sitting there nearly six months, we decided to leave and come back to the mainland, leaving the business (what business?) for sale and prayed someone would eventually be interested. The Post Office people were not best pleased, but my husband did not care anymore and could not wait to leave.

We decided to rent accommodation in Odiham, Hampshire, and after a search found a two up/two down terraced little house. We moved across the water exactly eighteen months after we arrived and spent Christmas 1986 licking our wounds.

We had no jobs, no home and my husband vowed he would never set foot again on the Isle of Wight.

In the winter of 1987, it was very cold and snow fell for weeks. I managed to get a job with Diners Club International in Farnborough. We sold our car and I travelled on the bus. My hours were erratic, as I was a telephonist, ringing people all over the world requesting they paid their Diners Club bills. I worked 10:00 a.m. to 6:00 p.m. one week and 6:00 p.m. to midnight the alternate week. They laid on a minibus for the late shift and I often walked four miles home in the bad weather. I had a good salary which just about kept us afloat with rent and living expenses, but my husband hated it, as it was the first time I was the breadwinner. He felt, I know, so inadequate and was depressed and moped around not knowing which way to go. I'm sure it was a very dark time for him. I again, bought Daltons Weekly to look for another enterprise. A dear friend lent us the money to buy a clapped out car, so we could view if anything turned up.

In March, I read re. a business like his first shop. It was in the south-west, an hour's journey from Bristol and just over an hour and a half to Plymouth, my mother's home, where she was born. I showed it to my husband and suggested there would be no harm in looking.

We journeyed down on a Sunday. The journey took just over two hours. I was impressed with the town, and the shop was in an arcade off the high street and the second biggest newsagents next to Smiths which was in the main thoroughfare.

My husband seemed interested and when we returned on the Monday, rang up for more information. It had twenty nine paper rounds and had been established many years with the present owner who was retiring.

The next big hurdle was finance and as there was no accommodation, somewhere to live! My husband approached two banks who were not helpful, but the next one we asked said they would like to see the books and they may consider it. He also asked if he could have an overdraft to put 10% down on a house. They were building on the outskirts of the town and we saw a small three bedroom house, which was fine and it would be great to have a home again.

Waiting for the decisions by the bank was agony and my husband could not be positive in view of the past.

To our relief, the bank was forthcoming and although it was a daunting project, having a mortgage over ten years because of our ages, at least my husband would be back in business, which he knew and liked. I would get a job and hopefully things and events would be brighter and more stable.

It was great to see my husband upbeat and enthused and although he did not say, our future happier and secure.

My husband moved into the business in April and I had to stay on at our rented house to fulfil the renting agreement. My husband lived in a room over a pub near his shop and motored up to see me most Sundays after the paper rounds were finished. He got up every morning at 5:30 a.m., collected the papers, marked them up and the paper boys (who were not always reliable) came in at 7:00 a.m. to deliver papers before going to school. Many times my husband did several rounds. He never complained, he was just glad he was back in business again.

I had to stay in the house in Hampshire for four months and although I did not like being separated, the time soon went by. The house we had purchased was in a small close and still being built.

It was a good day when I arrived, the same time as our furniture, to our brand new house, accompanied by two black poodles, Jolie and Jem. It was a bright, sunny day and I tried not to give a thought to the unhappy times in the past and hoped we had been given a third chance.

It was good to have familiar things around us. The garden was a challenge being new, but before long turf had been laid and it looked fine. I was so pleased for my husband and in a few months we bought another car and life seemed back to normality.

Our daughter visited and liked the change in her dad. He was more upbeat and enthusiastic. As usual he never discussed business and quite frankly I had given up asking, as the reply was always the same. I did not know whether it was pride or he did not think I was capable of understanding. I just don't know. We were happy and at the end of the year, even thought about a holiday in Spain with our friends, like we used to.

The close we lived in was very friendly and our neighbours first class.

One couple, he was a policeman on road traffic, the other side was a detached bungalow and a lovely couple who had retired. We made great friends with a couple opposite, approximately our age, with two grown-up children, had barbecues and went out for meals on a regular basis.

    I registered with an agency for an office job. For about a year I did several different jobs – switchboard in a factory environment, a solicitors office, a building society, a receptionist in a department store and what I liked best, working in the Crown Court in the Collections Office, taking fines etc. I eventually got a part-time job in a solicitors office off the high street. I was the oldest person working there and although I liked most of the staff, some were very patronising and referred to me as an old lady in her last job. I did not worry too much about it. I only wanted everything to be alright for my husband. He had part-time staff too – three ladies and himself. They all said he was a good boss to work for and business was fine, albeit hard, long hours, opening on Sundays, seven days a week. If there were papers to be delivered, you had to open. Sundays he closed at midday and he had Mondays off, as I did. I kept in touch with all our friends and a weekend in every month, we had visitors and we both liked entertaining. It seemed like old times when we lived in Surrey. The surrounding countryside was glorious and we were only half an hour from the sea. I once again applied for a Bench J.P. but unfortunately, they were well-pleased with a good register of magistrates, so my court work disappeared. I missed it very much and missed the camaraderie and meeting new people, doing something I liked and enjoyed. I wished I had pursued it earlier and even maybe become a legal executive and made a career out of the law.

    I do not think my husband realised how I felt and underestimated me re. business, but otherwise I was still in love with him and only wanted his best interests.

1988

We had that holiday and went to Estepona with our friends. It seemed all the bad old days were behind us and we had a lovely time. Went to Marbella many times, enjoyed long, lazy days on the beach. We rented a villa with a pool. It was grand. Went to Ronda where the first bullfight took place. I did not like the sport, but my husband and our friend did. The ladies went sightseeing and shopping!

We returned tanned and rested. All was well on our return and everything went back to normal.

Our daughter had the same boyfriend and we thought maybe this was the one. It seemed that all young people lived with their boyfriends and marriage was not the 'in thing'. She seemed happy and had done so well, going on a European tour with Tina Turner, doing her wigs and hair. She did not do the usual hairdressing, more a stylist, makeup and everything that goes with looking attractive. Although she had been away from home a long while, I still had withdrawal symptoms whenever she came to see us. Although I had many friends, she was my closest ally and I confided in her often, my worries about my husband and life in general.

I'm sure she often felt I was a 'silly billy' as unlike myself she was always laid back and like Scarlett O'Hara, tomorrow was another day. I admired this attitude. I know I worried unnecessarily, but that was my character and I have spoken to many sufferers and it's hard to come to terms with a demon that won't go away. I always wore my emotions near the surface. I was easily moved by events and felt sadness often. If someone told me an event that was heart-breaking, I felt too and sometimes could not shake it off like other people do.

1989 came and went. At the end of the year, I was stunned once again. My husband wanted to sell the business and buy a coffee shop in the town. I was disturbed by his decision. He just came home and said that was what he wanted to do. No discussion, just an ultimatum. Nothing I said would change his mind. The shop next door to ours was a successful coffee shop and he felt sure he could make a success of the same business. The shop he had seen was a secondary site, a walkway from the high street to a lovely church area in the town. It had been a café before, more a greasy spoon. My husband had great ideas, putting banquettes in, carpet and waitress service. Needless to say, I had great reservations about this and had visions of another disaster looming in our life. I just did not understand my husband's motives. He never seemed to be able to stabilise since his first business and the fire, and for the first time I was very hurt he did not talk to me and took no notice of consequences.

Dealing with the public and food is a totally different approach than a newsagents. A great deal of restrictions, health and safety issues, and the public very demanding. Nothing would change his mind. He maintained it would be much easier and not so demanding; getting up at 5:30 a.m., the newspaper rounds. In fact, he had nothing good to say about a business that had us on a good road, after the Post Office and house development. I thought it was folly and for the first time in our marriage, I resented his actions and thought he was only thinking it was what he wanted to do, regardless of the consequences, financially and the unknown.

Little did I realise what awful event would occur in 1991. I just had to go along with it and for the first time too, he called me a silly woman and why so pessimistic? I felt I had reason to be pessimistic, not silly.

Again, the newsagents sold quickly. The books were excellent. My husband had introduced good ideas. His staff were loyal and true. I felt very sorry for them as they were surprised and shocked. I asked him to see a financial adviser, but his mind was made up and I realised he did not want to listen to me or anyone.

After the purchase of the coffee shop went through, he gave himself a month to renovate. Again, I could not fault his hard work and on completion it looked first class. The décor was green and cream, green banquettes, green mottled wool carpet, a main counter with menu cards. He employed two part-time ladies – they wore dark green skirts and cream blouses. He did ask me re. its name which he wanted sign-written across the window that faced the street. After some thought, I suggested the name of our first poodle. His name was rather 'Dickens' in sound and association. He had a small fountain near the entrance with a lovely shrub in a decorative container. It was the first non-smoking coffee lounge in the town. On opening a reporter from the local newspaper gave it a good write-up. They were very busy. He sold baked potatoes with various fillings, cottage pie and lasagne, two soups of the day, various cakes and tea after 2:30 p.m. He opened at 8:30 a.m. and closed at 5:30 p.m. There were forty covers on the ground floor. There was a room upstairs suitable for parties and celebrations. Toilet facilities, and the kitchen with refrigeration and frozen food chests.

He had asked me to organise a licence for beers and spirits as I knew, being a J.P., the procedure. I went to the Crown Court. The Licensing Committee met every six weeks. It went through without a hitch. My name was above the door as the licensee. In hindsight it was not necessary, as no customer asked for that kind of refreshment, as it was essentially a coffee lounge. It was very well-presented and as always he had, I hoped, a winner. Always in the back of my mind were past dilemmas. My husband was now approaching sixty, the time when most people are hoping to wind down. This to me was another concern.

It was around this time that I felt my husband was drinking. He had always been a social drinker and most evenings had a whisky and a glass of wine at dinner. Often I could smell he had been drinking during the day and sometimes five evenings out of seven. Three whiskies followed by three quarters of a bottle of wine was consumed during the evening.

I felt if I said anything, I would be told not to be silly. After drinking most evenings he was asleep by 9:00 p.m. and I often went to bed alone. He would drive to the coffee shop and I knew if he had been stopped, the result would have been positive from the night before. I mentioned this, but it fell on stony ground, always accompanied by a remark that I did not want to hear.

I read in one of Winston Churchill's memoirs the following and I think it could apply:

"Men occasionally stumble over the truth, but most of them pick themselves up and hurry off as if nothing ever happened."

I confided in our doctor. He said of course he would help, but my husband would have to come to see him and want to change. I knew this would never happen and if I had asked him, he would have been very annoyed and retort the usual – silly woman.

I loved my husband dearly and just did not want people and myself to see this happening. I must admit the buzz I always felt when he was around did not happen anymore. I was constantly on edge and never knew what would happen from day to day. With the drinking came unkindness, bad behaviour, both to me and other people. I dreaded going out to social functions, dinners etc. I always insisted I drove the car. That was not easy as there were always caustic remarks about women drivers.

The coffee shop seemed to go forward. My husband never discussed it, as in the past. I felt after a while he was disenchanted with the running and daily routine. I just tried to take each day as it comes. My most important issue was my husband and prayed he would come to his senses.

It was now 1990. My husband's latest enterprise was still okay, as far as I knew. Always when his tax returns were due he would go into overdrive. He hated the admin and left everything to the last minute. Our lounge would be covered in paperwork which he seemed to take days and evenings to finish. He never seemed to visit his auditor and if he did he never said. In fact, I did not even know the company. If I had asked, I knew by experience he would not be forthcoming, saying he knew what he was doing.

I can believe that if you are told often enough that you are silly or stupid, you can begin to believe it. It demoralises you and you avoid any confrontation. It's easier.

To add to my worry, I felt that my husband may be interested in someone else.

The waitress staff were two forty-something ladies. I went into the coffee shop most mornings on my way to the office to have a hot chocolate or coffee. To my surprise, one of the employees from husband's news agency was waiting on customers. She had left the newsagents before my husband sold the premises. I knew she was not well-liked by the staff, coming and going as she pleased, and could be very sarcastic to customers and personnel. My husband knew this, but at the time took no notice, and her working at the coffee shop, to me, was surprising. She was not a people person and did not mix with the staff. Later, my husband's cook remarked she was trouble with a capital T.

When the evening came, I asked my husband why he had employed her again. His reply was first, it was none of my business, second, she had lost her job, and third, she was punctual and a good worker. I did not reply. I knew what he would say!

Over the following weeks, whenever I went into the coffee shop they would be sitting together laughing and talking quietly.

My husband did not come over and speak to me and one of the other staff would bring my coffee. I got more and more dismayed at this behaviour and confronted my husband one evening, before he started his usual drinking behaviour.

He was so annoyed. He said I was to apologise or else go to the doctor's as I was losing the plot. I felt so isolated. I could not talk to anyone and rather than he bully me, I agreed and said sorry. Nothing changed and unlike the rest of the staff, she wore jeans and a revealing blouse and appeared to rule the roost, sitting down reading the paper at every opportunity.

This year we did not have a holiday. I was relieved, as the friends we always went with would have been horrified at my husband's behaviour to me and his drinking.

The coffee shop seemed to tick over well and we now had a regular clientele who liked their surroundings and the food. During the summer months my husband put café tables and chairs outside which brought a continental feel to the coffee lounge and was well-received. It also had 'no smoking' – the first in the town – and this also was well-received, and of course is now widespread in restaurants, public houses etc.

In November our friends in Surrey invited us to a house party for Christmas. I wanted to go, but also dreaded it. My husband was not keen. For once he gave in and said it was just for two days, no longer.

We left on Christmas Eve. I drove as usual our car, a Toyota Corolla Automatic. I always enjoyed driving. Just as well in view of the strict drinking and driving was foremost at holiday times.

I wish there was a group for alcoholics' wives as well as AA, as life can be miserable and you just wish life could be like it used to be and you lose hope.

Our hosts were lovely people. Our host had his own business, totally different to ours. Nevertheless, all the responsibility for finance and staff. I was hoping I could drop a hint and hope he may have a talk with my husband about his fears and it may reveal an underlying reason for his behaviour.

It was not a merry Christmas – as soon as we arrived, approximately 7:00 p.m., he just helped himself to a large whisky, without being asked, consumed a lot of wine at dinner and continued afterwards. By Christmas Day, our hosts were aware of him drinking more than was acceptable. He did, I think, go out with the other lads who were attending after Christmas dinner and later my host told me he was going for broke. He hated the coffee shop environment, the place where he lived and so on. I could not say anything as my husband would have known I had spoken to him and it was a very sensitive issue between us. My husband was always good at putting on a façade and I do not think generally our daughter and indeed our friends could see these problems. I would have done anything to help. He shut me out and his lack of communication was evident re. his business, as it had always been in the past.

1990/1991

We arrived home, collected the dogs from the kennels, and life returned, as usual, to his drinking. Every evening he was asleep by 8:00 p.m. and most nights I went to bed alone and quite often I slept in our second bedroom as I did not sleep well, and his snoring did not help. I was beginning to feel unwell. My nerves shaky and I was always edgy, waiting for the next dilemma.

It did arrive, as in late March my husband announced one evening, he was selling the coffee shop. We were going through the whole scenario again after just eighteen months. This time he said he was retiring. I could not guess how my husband never saved money throughout our married life. He had no pensions. He always said the business was his pension. We had a large mortgage and outgoings to live. I just did not see how this could happen and I was frightened of the outcome. He would not accept any discussion and put it on the market. I asked every day if he had had any interest and after ten days, said there were two people who had viewed four times and he felt sure one was particularly interested. He asked me to remove my name as licensee, in case the next owner wanted to take it over. This was a formality. I went to the meeting of the Licensing Committee and asked for my name to be removed, as the premises were changing hands. I can remember on that particular day, I went into the shop to tell my husband that it had all gone well, sat down for a coffee and one of my husband's regular customers mentioned he was sorry we were leaving, retiring abroad, keeping a small apartment here to see our daughter. I did not say anything. In the evening I asked my husband why did the customer say this and once again he said I had misunderstood.

As regards what I thought was the other interest in his life, the person who worked for him. In February, St. Valentine's to be precise, my husband always brought me flowers, sent a card and we usually went out for dinner at our favourite watering hole, a wine bar in the town. We were good friends with the proprietors.

On 14th February 1991, this did not happen. My husband said we would go some other time, as he was going to a bank presentation for private pensions. There were no flowers or card. He left at 7:00 p.m. looking very smart. He asked for the car keys, always a dread. I asked him to have a taxi. He took no notice, said I'll see you later and left.

For the first time in our marriage, I checked up on what he had said. Next day, I rang the bank on another pretence and asked re. the previous evening. They did not know what I was talking about and assured me no such meeting had taken place. Although I was so upset, I almost knew that they would confirm my fears. Lying is not in my category and I felt sick.

I wanted to ask my husband, but I knew it would be to no avail, as he would turn it around and say I was the guilty party. From that time, I began not to believe anything he said.

Going back to my previous writing, March and going into April, very little was discussed re. the shop. He did say he hoped something was going to happen before June. I did not take a great deal of notice – except something odd happened. The person in question was no longer working at the coffee shop. When I enquired re. her absence, I was told by the staff she was getting married! This was an enormous relief and I asked my husband shall we buy a gift and he agreed. I bought a silver picture frame, wrapped it with a card. My husband said he would see she received it. I hoped, but it did not happen, a thank you, but I did not really care. I was just glad she had left. Many months later, I learnt this was a ploy and a lie to put me off the scent. She did not get married and had no intention to. I saw her around the town at different times – no wedding ring. The staff mentioned she regularly came into the shop and very often my husband would spend a whole afternoon away on the pretence he was at the cash and carry buying supplies for the shop. I spoke to our daughter re. my misgivings. It is now her great regret that she did not take it seriously, but said I was being oversensitive and her dad only ever wanted to be with me. Our daughter, living in London, did not see the full picture, although I had confided in her re. his drinking. She always said he would dust himself down and pick up and everything would be fine. It was just a bad phase or a midlife crisis.

In 1991 he was going to be sixty. A little late, I thought, but I don't know about these things. I do know this has crept into our society, as years ago you never heard about a midlife crisis. Like during the war, you had to grin and bear it and you did not have any choice.

In early April my husband asked me to take the books to an out-of-town location. I asked if they were his auditors. He said one of the viewing people were very interested. It was a private house and it did cross my mind, I always thought he dealt with a company. I'm sure the reader will think I was naïve, but always my husband kept all business matters almost secret, and in the past I had no reason to doubt his actions. I asked him why several times. It was always the same reply – he did not want me to be worried. I would reply, is there anything to worry about? He would shake his head. You are a silly billy. Matter closed. I agree I do get stressed out, but only if I'm kept in the dark. I would rather worry about what I did know than worry about what I do not know. He just did not understand that thinking and as I have said before, you give up trying.

I was so unhappy. I could not come to terms with the young man, who had come into my life at eighteen, overwhelmed me with love and affection, happy in our marriage, a lovely daughter, good living, caring and kind to a fault, was turning into someone I did not respect anymore and did not like.

You can't turn off thirty seven years of love and I still wanted it all to become right, but did not know how to make it happen – does anyone?

Nothing had been said re. what was going to happen when the coffee shop was sold. I had visions of my husband being at home all day, drinking or moaning re. his past mistakes, not trying to go forward and beat his demons.

I am now beginning to write in part three, what happened on May 2nd, knowing my life would never be the same again.

I feel I could write many more instances when I realised my husband was lying and being deceitful, but the reader would only find them repetitious and boring.

● * *

1991 – the third and last part of my true story

What happened in the last twenty two years has changed my attitudes, confidence and trust. I have come to realise that doors would have opened, if I had finance. The system we live under which I had always thought fair and just and would prevail, is not so. I am sure that the many events that happened to me were not believed by the general public and that is why I am writing this last phase, as they did happen and injustice was shown by people in authority – solicitors, barristers, and many more. Many people are treated this way. Only money speaks all languages and I feel this must be addressed, as it is grossly unfair and insurmountable in most cases.

May 2nd, 1991

It was a drizzly early morning with a slight promise of blue skies later on.

We got up, our usual time, 7:15 a.m. Not much was said as usual these days. After tea and toast, I took our two poodles for a short walk, whilst my husband shaved etc. He did suggest we went to supper that evening, which I was pleased, as I hoped he would tell me more about the shop and his decision to sell, and even maybe our future. I was aware he had become more withdrawn in the last fourteen days and hoped this may be a breakthrough to his silences. I drove the car, which was usual practice now, as I was always concerned re. my husband's drinking the evening before. He never questioned why I always drove. I think he was resigned to it or I hoped he knew the folly of driving. Even if he had drunk too much the night before, he just did not seem to care anymore.

I reversed out of the drive. At the end of the close one of our neighbours was standing waiting for a bus. I drove alongside the bus stop and offered her a lift into town. She was pleased, as she had just missed the bus and had another twenty minute wait.

My husband got into the back seat and she sat in the passenger seat, next to me.

We talked about anything and everything, mainly the weather, which is our usual conversation us Brits are pre-occupied with.

It took only ten minutes to reach the town centre. I stopped to let our neighbour off first, asking my husband where he wanted to go. His coffee shop was in a non-traffic walkway off the high road. He suggested a large car park – he could walk through a short covered way into the high street, across the road into the corridor that ran through to another car park and Church Square.

He got out of the car, never said goodbye or kissed me. I watched him walk down a ramp into the car park. He never turned and waved, which he usually did. I sighed, put the car into gear and drove down the Crescent and found a space near the exit of the church car park. I always reversed into a space, as we had an agreement – leaving the ignition key in a black key wallet on the back wheel, so it could not be seen from the front. This was because he sometimes went to the cash and carry during the day. I was in no hurry. Walked to Boots and then carried on the main street, looking in the windows of the shops. Arrived at the office, picked up the post, put it into the appropriate named slots, turned the small switchboard onto manual, sat down and waited for the calls that came in fast and furious after 9:30 a.m.

It was a Thursday. We were not terribly busy. I made coffee for everyone, did some filing, tidied up numerous papers, chatted to clients who were waiting to be seen. The morning went fairly quickly. As it was still raining I decided to get a sandwich and have my third cup of coffee and stay in during my lunch hour. The staff room was not very big and was not used much, as most of the staff had lunch in a nearby public house. The staff were not the friendliest lot. It did not concern me, as I worked part-time. I just had contact with the young woman who did the other hours. The secretaries were on the first floor and would wave on their way out. I rarely had contact with them, only on the telephone. The men staff rarely chatted or even said hello – I have worked in a more friendly environment. The clients were the most pleasant and that suited me.

I usually finished at 3:30 p.m. and switched the small switchboard over to automatic, said farewell and left. On this particular day, the big white chief asked me to stay on until 4:15 p.m. It was no problem. I just liked to get home so I could take the dogs for a good walk. It was fine as I had booked our supper for 7:30 p.m. and there was plenty of time.

I left, walked to the car park, got into the car. On the passenger seat, a pair of shoes in a brown bag. I had asked my husband to collect them from the repairers.

The traffic was not heavy. I arrived home at about 4:40 p.m.

As I drove onto the drive, I noticed my two dogs were sitting on the window sill. I thought it was odd, as they slept in the utility room when we were out. I momentarily thought my husband was home as he often came by taxi or walked and left the staff to shut the shop at 5:00 p.m.

I should have known otherwise, as he would not have allowed the dogs to go onto the furniture and onto the window sill. Nevertheless, I called his name. There was no reply. The dogs were demanding attention around my ankles. I let them out into the garden. It was now quite pleasant and the temperature good. I watched the dogs race around the garden and went to look at the pool, to see if the heron had called. All was well, I'm glad to say.

I went into the kitchen, filled the kettle. Whilst I was running the water, on the draining board I noticed an envelope with my name on it. I put the kettle down, picked up the envelope. It was not sealed. I opened it and read the content. I realised after a few minutes I was still holding it and I was on the floor. It read:

My name,

I have gone for broke. Think of me as dead. That's the best for everyone. Take care and love our daughter. Forgive me.

Forever and always,

His name

I read it over and over again. My mind was racing. I went into the lounge and just kept saying, it can't be true. I do not know how many times I read the letter. I was so bewildered. I rang my friend I shared my job with and just said please come. She told me she knew by my voice it was serious and did not ask any questions. Her journey would have taken fifteen minutes. I cannot remember my waiting. I just kept saying out loud, please come back.

My friend arrived, read the letter and said you must ring the police. I asked her to make the call. They were knocking on the door in ten minutes. My friend tried to make me drink a brandy and tea, but I was uncontrollably shaking in the upper part of my body, especially my arms.

I knew the police were speaking to me and I was answering, but it seemed in the distance and I could not hear myself. I felt I was acutely hard of hearing in myself and not to other people. It's hard to explain. I thought my heart was coming out of my chest and I could not stop shaking. I wanted to cry, but nothing happened. My doctor told me later that I was having an acute panic attack and at later times, I experienced this very often.

The police asked for a photograph of my husband and also I told them he was not mobile as I had our only car. At this time, I had not gone upstairs. My friend helped me to the bottom of the stairs and followed behind. As I came level with the landing, I noticed the loft ladder was down and a pair of rolled up socks on the landing. I went into our third bedroom – we used it as a dressing room. The fitted wardrobe doors were swung open. One jacket on a hanger, everything else was empty. I went into our bedroom. It looked as if we had been burgled. My jewellery case was open and most of the items gone. Our bed had obviously had a suitcase on it. The place was very untidy. It immediately made me realise that someone who takes their life does not take his clothes etc. My friend gasped and said my name with emphasis. I did not know what to feel – relief or anger. My emotions were everywhere. I just remembered being very sick and the shaking much worse. I took a photograph and went downstairs. The police said it would be released on TV after the news, and as soon as they knew anything would be in touch. I told them about the clothes and said my husband must have a case.

My friend rang home and said she would stay with me overnight and would her husband bring toiletries etc. I wanted to speak, but all I could say is, He will come back, this is all a mistake.

My friend rang my daughter the same evening and she said she would come on the first train from Paddington. She did not enlarge on what had happened, just said something serious had happened re. her father. I laid down on our bed, did not undress. My thoughts were racing. I hardly slept. My friend left for the office at 8:45 a.m. and said she would ring me during the morning. I cannot remember how I made the journey to the train station. I seemed to be in automatic and did things without knowing. I still felt very shaky and not able to relate to normal sounds and happenings. I constantly kept saying to myself, He will come back. When I met my girlie at the station, I clung to her and could not say anything. The journey home was quiet and it was not until I got indoors, showing her the letter that we started to communicate. I once again started the involuntary shaking. She was dumbstruck and like me said it's all a mistake and it will come right. Unlike me, she said we must be realistic and see how my financial situation was! Plus the shop staff should be notified. I gave her the shop number. I heard her talking.

She came into the lounge ashen faced. "Mummy, the shop was sold on the 22nd April." Where had Dad been going for the last ten days? Also, the new owner wanted to see me, as he had several serious concerns, about money. He said the staff had not been paid for three weeks and there were several outstanding debts that had been brought to his notice. Non-payment of hire purchase on microwaves and refrigeration which my husband had agreed to settle on completion of the sale.

In the following weeks, I could write forever what was revealed. My husband had committed fraud on two occasions involving me and our daughter. He had re-mortgaged the house on two occasions to the amount of £40,000, forging both my daughter's and my name, showing a letter of consent from me as I was in hospital having special treatment, which of course was completely untrue. He had not paid the mortgage for nine months, always the excuse when he sold his business he would be able to pay his debts. Deception was very evident. Taking out loans, supposedly for a car, he had overdrafts at two banks. Another revelation found by the police – he had changed his name, taking out other loans, Barclaycards and American Express and running them side by side. The police presumed this had been going on for approximately a year before he left. One must remember in 1991, there were no check-ups, pin numbers etc. and although I am sure one gets frustrated with security now, this could not happen now.

Needless to say, I was completely bewildered. I'm sure this is why his drinking had escalated; the mood swings and unpleasantness. I began to think I was not married to the same man. I seemed to spend every day apologising and feeling so betrayed.

He also owed money to several people – renovations of the coffee shop, workmen, the local butcher for produce in the coffee shop, his baker's bill had run up to over £400. He even sold pictures in the shop, brought in by an artist who he had befriended and never saw any of the money. This was classified as theft and taking money under false pretences.

Our daughter, like me, was devastated and made a record of his misdemeanours. We just did not know what to do. There was no money for a solicitor. We were in limbo!

At the peak of all this turmoil, I received a letter from our building society, saying in six weeks' time I would be homeless. The house was being repossessed. The contents would also be taken against outstanding monies and an inventory would be taken, as I had no financial means of support.

On average I had a panic attack most days and the shaking was permanent it seemed. I was even asked if I was suffering from Parkinson's disease.

I asked the police if they could find how my husband had left without being mobile. They were not very enthusiastic and said they were assured there was no foul play and anyone is allowed to leave. My thoughts were if he was mobile, perhaps he could be traced and made to face all his misdemeanours. Nevertheless, they said they would look into the situation.

There was no let up for me. People ringing up wanting their money and I'm sure not believing I knew anything about it and what he had been up to.

The police returned after forty eight hours with yet another revelation – my husband had stolen a car!

It transpired he had visited a Renault garage several times on the outskirts of the town, asked if he could test drive a new car, showing he was well-known at the Chamber of Commerce and a local businessman. They had allowed him to go unaccompanied as all their representatives were busy or unavailable. He took the car and never returned.

The police thought he had put the car in private garaging, driven to our home on the day, filled the car with his belongings – books, all his VAT returns, DIY tools etc. – and left.

Our neighbour who was a traffic policeman verified on the afternoon in question, he and his wife did remark there was a car on the drive and they thought we had visitors. The car was backed up to open garage doors and no doubt he was partially hidden from passers-by and could load it unobserved, remembering we lived in a cul-de-sac and most of them were at work, so it would be easy for this to take place.

The police said the car's value was £18,000, brown in colour and non-registered number plates. Later it was revealed the car had left Portsmouth early on the following day, Friday, for Cherbourg.

Immediately, the garage and car company alerted agents in Europe that the car was stolen and should be apprehended as the driver was wanted for theft and questioning about other matters.

I felt so ashamed for my husband. How could this happen? The kind, loving, young man I had married had become a thief and many other things. A totally dishonourable man. I found it so hard to acknowledge these events. I felt I was in a very dark place. Hopelessness was in my mind. I had no money, my home was going to be taken away, he had abandoned not only me, our daughter as well. She was constantly propping me up, but inside suffering so much, realising her father's failings and being betrayed and rejected. Men will always leave their wives, not your children. I would rather see my daughter ten minutes in a year than never again. It was a cruel action and one I find unforgiveable.

The police, I felt, were very flippant, saying once there is no indication of foul play, the file goes on the shelf! One officer even said: "He has been a naughty boy. They usually come back and say sorry and it will be okay." I did not think much of their so-called 'help' and understanding.

My daughter's main concern was I was losing my home in a few weeks. She had stayed with me for fourteen days, but being freelance had to get back or else she would be in financial trouble. She reassured me at every opportunity that she would look into obtaining a mortgage, so perhaps we could find accommodation and I would not be homeless. Although a friend had kindly offered me a room, this had no future, as I could not stay indefinitely. Social Services were not helpful, saying I could go into a hostel or bed & breakfast. I felt so isolated and still trying to come to terms with my husband's actions.

We had an appointment with C.A.B. They listened, but said they had not heard of something so bizarre and could give me no direction as what to do. They suggested I went to a solicitor's surgery, but this all takes time and I did not have that luxury.

I hope the reader will forgive me, as my writing is haphazard. So much was in my mind at this time. Emotionally, I was a wreck. Trying to come to terms with my husband's absence, not knowing where to turn re. finance, losing my home etc. My daughter was marvellous, always reassuring me. I was always asking questions, for which there were no answers, as she was, like me, bewildered. I really thought at times, I was losing my mind.

My doctor was a real ally, but could only prop me up with dealing with my stress and panic attacks. I was reluctant to take pills and maybe become dependent. I had lost two stone in a very short time. I was not eating very much, I rarely went shopping due to lack of funds. I was also losing my car, as it was on HP and I knew it was in arrears, like everything else.

What I could not get my head around was how did my husband think I would cope? The lack of care was overwhelming.

A friend gave me the local newspaper to see if there were any rooms or small flats available. The council had said they would give thought to housing benefit if anything came available. Having dogs could be a problem.

I saw an advert for a terraced property – two up/two down, bathroom and kitchen, being built in a village two miles from the town. My biggest problem other than money was getting accommodation that would allow dogs, as I was determined to keep them in my life, as I had little else.

A friend took me out to the site. There was one left – an end of terrace. I rang my daughter and she said I'll come down and we will have a look. I was told by my solicitor many months later that if I had gone to a solicitor, he would have written to the building society asking to hold off repossession until I had sold the house. Being evicted I had a CCJ against me which, if in the future I had wanted a loan, my credit rating would be affected. No one told me this and as I did not have funds, I could not afford a solicitor! So I lost my home.

My daughter said she thought everything would be okay and set the wheels in motion to buy it on my behalf. She paid a holding fee on the house and we waited with baited breath.

The day arrived when I left my house of four years. The bailiffs had taken an inventory of the contents. I was allowed to keep my two-seater sofa, a chair, bed and two changes of bed linen, clothes, and three sentimental ornaments my parents had given us.

They took all the white kitchen furniture – microwave, washing machine, dishwasher, video – leaving the TV. They cut the carpets up, my lovely velvet curtains, rugs, and I could not believe it, my dog baskets, books, pictures. What was left, very little, was housed in a portacabin I had rented for £10 per week, under a flyover in the town. Several months later, it was vandalised and set fire to, so that was the end of a life for me. I had got past caring and just wanted to survive.

It took two and a half months for the house project to be finalised. I'll never be able to put into words my gratitude to my girlie.

Unfortunately, it was short-lived.

The powers that be gave me a little housing benefit which I gave to my daughter for the mortgage repayments. I was two years off my old age pension, so I decided I must get some income. I had never returned to work and being two years off sixty, no one was interested in employing me. I must admit my concentration levels were very poor, as there were still more revelations re. my husband's actions. I put three cards in the Post Office saying I was available for cleaning and ironing.

Within one week, I had two jobs – one cleaning a large house for a lady who was a head teacher at a local school. She was very kind and knowing my situation, let me do my laundry at her house. She moved during the time I was with her and I was included. I did errands and she always reimbursed me. We are still good friends. She has now retired and lives on the Devon coast enjoying her retirement near her family, and which she justly deserves.

The other person was not so good. I did ironing for five hours without a break, every Thursday. It was mostly heavy bed linen. She insisted on the towels, socks, everything, and some of it unnecessary. The room was cold on a stone floor. I rarely saw my employer. She left money every week whether I did two basketfuls or six.

Later, I did find it a little easier, as two good friends bought me an old Toyota car which made life not so hectic, catching buses etc. My money went towards outgoings and most of it on trying to manage. Some weeks I did not have enough petrol and I used to walk to do my work.

I did not feel secure, even though I had a roof over my head and I felt I would never feel secure again. I was still trying to come to terms with my husband's disappearance. Not a week went by, something more came out of the woodwork. The new owner of the coffee shop was taking me to court, saying I was involved in the plot and the money that was involved. Also, evidently, my husband had given wrong accounts re. the business and various other issues. I used to dread the post, and the doctor said I was near to a nervous breakdown. I realise now, I still fantasised that my husband would come back and sort it all out.

I have forgotten to say earlier, another awful event.

I had my own account at a building society where I had put my salary. It had a four figure amount in the account. I said to my daughter, at least I had some money of my own. She accompanied me to the office. I requested to remove the monies and close the account. After waiting ten minutes, a young woman returned to say the account had already been closed! He had once again produced a letter with my signature, fraudulently of course, saying I was in hospital and unable to come in to close the account, as we were going to retire and live abroad. He also said he had a business in the town and he was a member of the Chamber of Commerce.

After visiting the building society, we found from the local newspaper a solicitor's surgery. I wanted to know if I could take action, as even with a typewritten letter with my forged signature, should have been more watchful and the society should not have given my husband the funds which belonged to me.

The solicitor listened and said I would not get Legal Aid as it was a civil matter. Yet again, I feel, so unjust. I never received any apology re. this matter. I had become a victim yet again and I reiterate money was the injustice of the matter. Time and time again this occurred and I just could not overcome these hurdles.

Every time another revelation, after the initial shock, I just could not get my head around the deviousness and what I would have to cope with – the humiliation and also feeling so foolish.

Of course the employees were also taken in, but if something like that had transpired when I was employed, it would have been looked into and steps taken, but nothing was investigated and my money had been taken under false pretences. Once again, I reiterate, if I had funds, steps would have been taken. My daughter was furious as we had nowhere to go. The hopelessness.

The day I left my home was one of the saddest days. I stood on the drive, seeing all my life with my husband disappear. Everyone, including the bailiffs, tried to console me. Deep down I have always found it very hard and I feel damaged and healing still taking place after twenty years. I wished every day that my parents were around to give me support and their love. I'm pleased they are not, as my father would have been so angry, mainly so disappointed at my husband's behaviour, as he always said he was the son he never had and he loved him.

I tried to manage my emotions. The evenings were always my hardest time. I would sit and think. Go over events and always the disbelief at my husband not caring what happened to me and my life.

Living in my little house still did not do anything to my need of security. It was very difficult to manage our finance from my two jobs. My daughter propped me up on numerous occasions. She was paying the mortgage which was demanding on her. She had her own expenses and living in London has never been easy financially. She was marvellous and I will never be able to put in words, her support emotionally and financially. I was wishing the time away, for my old age pension in two years. Not that it would be great, as I had only worked since my daughter's fifteenth birthday and then only paid my stamp on part-time employment. Anything would be helpful.

I used to get very irritated by people who I know cared, saying 'time will heal'. It has not. 'Look forward.' What had I to look forward to? 'There's a light at the end of the tunnel.' I don't think so, and no one knows how one feels, unless they have been there. Everyone is different in reaction and although I was not lonely, I felt very alone, and at times desperate.

After one year, since my husband's absence, I had no credit rating and several CCJs against me from people my husband had taken their money. We were partners on paper with the coffee shop and people were always hoping money would come from me. They of course were unaware, I had received no monies from our house and an old-fashioned word – destitute!

In late October, a good friend telephoned me. At a dinner party, a friend of hers said she had seen my husband in a resort in Portugal, giving out timeshare leaflets. She remembered him from a dinner party we had attended years before.

She had taken it upon herself to locate the company whilst she was staying there. My friend was passing the information on to me.

I found out the telephone number through International Directory and after a lot of heart-searching, decided to telephone, with a view, talking to him.

It took me forty eight hours to compose myself and what I was going to say. Due to the time difference I decided to ring at 11:00 a.m. At the first try, I got no response, as he was not in the offices. They told me he would be there the next day in their office, as there was a meeting of representatives. I spent a sleepless night, wondering what my call would bring.

I again telephoned and this time, I heard my husband's voice. I asked him, please do not ring off and begged him to come back and everything was in such chaos. He said he would think about it. No apology or enquiry after our daughter and the circumstances we were in. He did say he would get a prison sentence and he just did not know what to do! Also, he would telephone me after forty eight hours and talk to me again. I could tell from his voice, he was shocked I had traced him, but did not ask how!

Needless to say, he never called and after three days, I again rang the timeshare office and was told he had left very quickly and left no forwarding address. That was the last time I heard his voice.

In hindsight, I should have gone to the resort myself to confront him, but as always funds were not available and I would have had to borrow same. My emotions were in rags, as obviously there was no remorse. I felt desolate. His running away again was so cowardly and uncaring. I wrote to the head office of the timeshare company asking if he had transferred elsewhere. After six weeks they replied. They had no information re. his whereabouts and once more, it all came to nothing.

Again, late that year, it was revealed my husband had taken out a private pension plan. He receives this and I write every year to see if it is in place and due to the Data Protection Act, they give no information. I wish there was a law that protected me. Again, injustice.

Sometimes they reply, but more than often, I never get an acknowledgement. I have pointed out that the Data Protection Act is null and void if the person is deceased and as now he is nearly eighty two, this would bring closure. As usual no one seems to care and I find that very hard. As the victim, this no fault of my own.

The months turned into another year and although I was settled in my little house, I was still being plagued by people my husband owed money to.

The building society did not let up and although the house had sold, the outstanding remortgage my husband had made was still very much alive. My daughter and I had numerous interviews at head office in London which took its toll moneywise. We also reiterated what had happened on each occasion. They did not seem to comprehend my situation. They requested a token payment each month and if my circumstances changed, they would review. I explained that was highly unlikely, as the only monies I was going to receive was my old age pension in eighteen months' time. The interviews were very stressful, as we were put in separate rooms to see if we both gave the series of events. It was like being treated as a criminal at a police station.

They said I must make more of an effort to find my husband and patronising in manner, asked me to try the Red Cross or Salvation Army. I had of course already done that, but pointed out they do not make enquiries for nothing. I did not know and maybe the general public are unaware, if they do locate the person, the person can request their whereabouts are not given. The Red Cross and Salvation Army are duty-bound to honour same. Again, such injustice. There must be hundreds of people trying to find loved ones and getting nowhere. The law seems, yet again, unfair and one-sided.

My husband had now been gone seventeen months. Things had died down. The building society made enquiries re. my situation, regularly, getting a letter every month! People stopped me in the street to ask questions and now I had no credit facilities and my credit rating was nil. I had one store card, but nothing outstanding. My pension would be available in another four months, not that I knew how much. Anything would be a bonus.

My doctor still saw me every month. He insisted my panic attacks seemed to have come to stay and he was also very concerned re. my mental health. I could not concentrate for very long and could not read a book at all, had no interest. I had lost three stone in weight. I hope the reader will understand, there was no light-heartedness in me, which made me dull and uninterested. On one visit, my doctor suggested I see a counsellor. In hindsight, the best of suggestions. She was a charming lady. A good listener, of course, with a more positive approach, rather than an emotional one. My main issue was my husband's lack of care, what happened to me. She explained that many people just blot out events, thinking only of themselves and saving their own skin. She related to me how she knew one lady who had gone through the same thing and her husband turned up sixteen years later, as if nothing had happened. She also suggested I join a group, all who had missing people in their lives and then I would not feel so isolated and alone. The main idea she put forward was to join as a volunteer in some good works, leaving the decision to me – what group?

A few weeks later, a friend gave me the local paper. Usually full of births, engagements and death announcements, cinema schedules and local crime. In a box tucked away on the last page, a request for people to become supporters in the charity Victim Support. I immediately related to this, because of my circumstances. There was a meeting arranged in the police station, 2:00 p.m. on the following Wednesday afternoon.

I went along. There were only eleven people there – two men and the rest female.

A police officer and a member of the charity gave a very interesting account of the support group they wanted. There would be a six week training scheme at the police college in another town. When completed, assessments and appraisals made as to what you were most suited to.

The lectures and talks were very informative. There were videos and mock court sessions, a Crown Court visit and discussions with clerks, judges and other court personnel. I liked it, as it brought back memories of my magistrate involvement and procedures.

At the end of the training, four were selected out of the eleven: myself, two other ladies and one gentleman. Several of the participants felt they could not cope with many harrowing details shown.

Our contact was through the police and we also had a small office in the courthouse with an adviser if you needed advice.

The adviser had asked if I would like to choose a support for small children, up to the age of eleven. I like children very much, finding them more honest and giving, unlikely to be devious, sly and untruthful than adults. I was very pleased to have been asked and within six months, the police were asking for me, as the children liked me and their parents felt comfortable and reassured when I met them and their families. It was just before the evidence could be given through videolink. The parents are not allowed with children either in court or the videolink room. You, the supporter, are in attendance at all times, to guide and make the ordeal as painless as possible. On average, the evidence takes over twelve months to be accepted by the CPS, before it comes into court. The supporter goes to the home or care home and befriends the child and the family, gains their confidence and becomes a friend, organising a court visit in an empty court and on most occasions the judge who will be residing, and on the day of the court sitting, the prosecution and defence, solicitors or barristers that will be there on the day, thus putting the child at ease.

A court visit for an adult is very stressful. Imagine what it can be for a child, relating what happened.

Sadly, most child appearances are for mental, physical or sexual abuse and invariably this has been by a relative or someone close to the child and its family, making it more frightening and embarrassing for the family.

Generally, the children were charming, bewildered and unsure of course, easy to get to know. Years ago, children were not believed in court cases, thought to tell lies and fantasise. Thank goodness, it is now much improved. Screens can be requested if the child is in court or the videolink room. The children's parents are not allowed in the room, only myself and the child, sometimes accompanied by an usher of the court.

I always insisted that the little person may be allowed to bring their favourite toy or toys. I always read 'The Velveteen Rabbit' book. There is an excellent moral in between its pages. A drink and of course chocolate or sweets. I was known as the 'Teddy Bear Lady', as I always gave my charge a bear for bravery. I kept a little book and asked them to put their birthday date and my telephone number for their parents if they felt unhappy about anything. I was never allowed to enquire what had happened. If the child told me anything I thought was relevant, I would inform the police. Only once in thirteen years did I have one child say they were lying, because it got people into trouble. Unlike adults, children are more honest and forthcoming. Adults are devious, cunning and liars.

I was also asked to join the management committee and met many interesting people. This involvement put my own troubles to the back of my mind, temporarily.

Due to the contacts I made, at last, I was put in touch with a lady solicitor, out of town, who promised to look into my husband's affairs before he left.

I was granted legal aid which, of course, I could not have proceeded without financial help.

Many issues came to light – a private pension, tax evasion, and many more.

The solicitor used a private agent and so much was revealed. My husband had obviously been planning his getaway, for two years. He had changed his name, legally to his mother's maiden name. I think I have mentioned this before – it is very important as he was having a double life.

The first thing my solicitor advised was for me to change my married name and I decided to do so and reverted to my maiden name. I felt there was no honour in having his name anymore.

I was fast coming to 1993, when I would receive my old age pension. I hoped it would ease my ongoing anxiety re. my funds. Fortunately, through the court, I had befriended people with young children and I offered my time to babysit. This was very popular for me and within a year, I had a clientele of five families who requested my time, especially at Christmas and holidays. In fact, I gave up my five hour ironing job, as I developed spondylosis in my neck and shoulders. Later, I also had to cope with chronic arthritis everywhere. It was a lonely job when the children had gone to bed, but it was very pleasant to sit in a warm house, with coffee if I wanted it and having a chat with parents, who became friends.

The solicitor used my legal aid to hire an enquiry agent and after six weeks, many more issues came to light re. my husband.

So much money he had taken under false pretences. He had organised an auditor to alter his books, as the coffee shop was not making any money, as he was always fobbing off people he owed money to by saying he would pay on the sale of the shop which, of course, was untrue, as he took a very large amount with him. I could write many pages, but I'm sure the reader would find it bewildering and bizarre.

My hopes of him ever returning were now dim, but I thought of him every day, hoping his conscience would realise what he had done. My counsellor said people can block out things they know are wrong. Of course, she was right.

I believe Churchill said: "Most men know they have done wrong, but dismiss it and just hurry on to the next subject in their lives."

At least she was able to write to people saying I was no way involved and the police had completely exonerated me. The people usually replied, saying that if my husband returned, they insisted they were informed. The only group who did not accept were the building society and for the next three years, I was constantly bombarded with threatening letters and was interviewed numerous times. Always seeing a different person, so I had to go through the whole events again and again. They did not show any understanding at all. It was always money, money, and another five letter word came to mind, beginning with G: Greed.

The months went into years. I enjoyed my Victim Support work, rarely went out except for babysitting and cleaning. My little dog Gemmy died and I felt more lonely than ever. After a lot of deliberation, I did not look around for another dog. Poodles were still costly to have and keep.

In 1996, I had a nasty health setback. I was diagnosed with Ménière's disease. Not life-threatening, but it threatens your life. I was in hospital a week after losing my balance and falling down a flight of stairs. I fractured my arm, but doctors were more concerned why I had lost my balance. The other symptoms were violent sickness, giddiness and loss of hearing. I had not investigated the disease, but I had heard of it. Stress was another factor and I had that in bowl fulls. You can go months without an attack, which I did.

After leaving Virginia Orchard, I moved into one room in a village called Corfe. I lived there in a friend's house for nine months altogether which I was very grateful for. After this time I moved to Cann Street, Taunton and lived there for two years.

In early 1997, I was having an attack once a month. I would have to go to bed in a semi-dark room. Sometimes it lasted hours, other times days. I invested in a magazine called 'Spin', the Ménière's Society's quarterly magazine. It included a mailing list of other sufferers. No two sufferers had the same symptoms and doctors knew very little re. the cause. The ear being the smallest organ in your body and rarely penetrated was a mystery.

I decided to make contact with other sufferers in the county with a view to starting a group, meeting once a month, and discussing our different approaches to the disease, its unpredictability and self-help. I advertised in the newspaper and was overwhelmed by people ringing up and saying how interested they were.

Our first meeting brought forward twenty three people with Ménière's. Everyone was very enthusiastic. We decided on a subscription which went to the Ménière's Society and hopefully fundraising. Ménière's has a very low image and we hoped to bring the condition to the public's notice.

Within six months, our group had grown in stature and the society informed us, we were a leading light re. the disease, and many more groups were formed over the country. I was the spokesperson for the county I lived in and other groups did the same. I was the contact person to give news, fundraising etc.

The group had been in place nearly four years and we had collected over one thousand pounds for the charity.

I decided rightly or wrongly to stand down and pass the baton on to another member. After this time, one runs out of ideas and feels jaded, so when I announced my decision at the AGM, I was very dismayed that no one would carry the banner for Ménière's. Unfortunately, there were internal politics. The secretary and treasurer decided also to resign and after two months of trying to find a chair etc., the group was disbanded. Head office were very despondent, as I was. Sometimes it is very difficult to pass on enthusiasm and dedication. I am still the contact for the county and give talks on Ménière's for fundraising.

In 2002, I was still having attacks, back to back, and after suffering four months in this state, my doctor referred me to an ear, nose and throat specialist, who recommended an operation. My balance nerve to my left ear was cut and I had an injection of Gentamicin with a plug in my ear for ten days. It was then removed surgically. I waited with baited breath to see if my condition improved! After one more attack shortly after removal of the plug, I have only had four attacks. My balance has suffered severely, but I have done exercises and walk outside with a stick. Life is much more easy and I am very grateful to my surgeon. Few people have surgery, so I recommend it whenever possible. Ménière's is incurable as doctors do not know the cause. Many suggestions have been put forward: a salt-free diet, decaffeinated tea and coffee, and the three Cs – cheese, coffee and chocolate – and also a key factor, stress. I always took a survey of new members in the group and stress appeared more than anything else, and lifestyle. I will always be on medication for Ménière's; a form of antihistamine and a tablet for sickness and vertigo.

I enjoyed very much bringing Ménière's to the public whenever I could and I will always be interested to hear if research brings relief to the many sufferers who have to go through life with this very distressing condition.

In 1998, a happy/sad event took place.

In late June, my daughter came down from London for a three day visit. I met her at the station and by the time we got to the car park, she told me she was getting married on July 22nd at 12 noon.

Her excitement was catching. I was so pleased, but disappointed I could not contribute to the arrangements, like most mothers of the bride.

The service was going to be in Chelsea, and afterwards a small lunch party at Topo Gigio's restaurant in Brewer Street. She had made all the plans so that I would not fret over wishing I could have done more – the dress, wedding cake, photos etc.

They were having a friends reception later on her birthday, a month later.

The 22nd July was a lovely sunny day. I went to stay at my cousin's in Pinner the day before.

Promptly at 11:15 a.m. a car arrived to take me to the wedding. We were meeting in Chelsea for the service and afterwards all go together to the lunch.

My daughter looking very pretty in a lilac dress and strappy sandals. Her hair looked lovely piled high on her head and catching the sunlight in her highlights, and happiness on her face was very evident. She had a bouquet of cream flowers and there were flowers, profuse everywhere.

They had their own vows, along with the seriousness of the service and all was well.

I know I smiled a lot, as I liked my son-in-law very much, but there was an ache in my heart that her dad was absent on a very important day for any girl. My emotions were varied – resentment, deep sadness and many unfulfilled wishes.

Later, unbeknown to our daughter, I advertised in the Daily Telegraph for a week, in the personal column, telling my husband of our daughter's marriage and hoping he would at least send a card to the box number. I did this as he always read the Telegraph on holidays etc., but needless to say, nothing came of my wish.

My daughter never referred to his absence, but I know in my heart and hers, the thought was there.

This writing will be the first time she has known of my action and I hope she will understand my feelings.

They were married on a Wednesday and stayed the night at a boutique hotel in Soho. I have plenty of photographs and had a collage made up and framed for me to look at and remember.

The Millennium – 2000
A good turning point in my life on my own.

In late May, a long-time friend's daughter invited me to my friend's seventieth birthday in Ashburton, Devon. She booked me into a B&B, nearby the venue. I decided to drive down in a better car I had now acquired with a loan from a friend. The lady in question was with me all those years ago when I met my husband in the cinema in 1950, Christmas. We had always kept in touch, after I was married. She lived in Middlesex for four more years when a tragedy happened. Her mother was killed in an accident on the A30. The backdraught of a lorry knocked her off her bicycle and she was killed. My friend decided to return home to care for her father and brother. Her father remarried after a few years. He left her the family home and moved a few miles away.

She married when she was forty, to a Yorkshire gentleman, a widower, quite a few years older. They had a daughter the following year, who had sent me the invitation. It was all meant to be a surprise and truly was. There were over eighty people who attended and my friend's breath was a gasp when she saw all her friends, many since childhood, school, but only me from her life in London. It was a great evening and as I rarely socialised these days, a real treat for me.

I spent the Sunday with my friend and her family. We had a barbecue in their garden – it was grand. Needless to say, we became nostalgic and talked about all the happy times in our youth. My friend was devastated re. my husband and just could not understand why, when we had been such a happy couple.

I returned home on the Monday and as always there was post and junk mail on the hall floor.

I made a cup of tea, fed my little dog, who also had enjoyed plenty of petting and cuddles. I had given in to having a dog and besides, I was missing having to come back to an empty house and got another little 'café au lait' poodle. She was really a rescue, as her owner was retiring through ill health and moving her dogs on. I called her Kirie. She was very highly strung and did not take to training well, but I loved her and she was always by my side and very affectionate.

Back to the post on return from my friend's happy birthday. As always, several window envelopes, junk mail and one official-looking white envelope addressed To Whom It May Concern. I opened it with no concern. On reading it, news at last re. the council finding me a home. They were offering a one bedroom bungalow in the village I had lived in when my daughter bought me the little house after my husband left. I read the letter many times. I had to view the property within twenty four hours and make up my mind within twenty four hours, otherwise the property would be offered to the next person on the waiting list. I could collect the keys from the council offices and view the bungalow.

I telephoned right away and said I would be there as soon as possible. I asked directions to the property and held my breath. It was nine years since my husband had gone and three moves later, I was being offered a home I would not have to worry about at last and more importantly, I could live out the rest of my life.

I went to the bungalow the next day. I felt nervous as I had never had to make a decision of this calibre, so I must think wisely before making a decision. The alternative was maybe waiting many more years and thinking of my advancing years and not having to depend on my daughter, this was a very important decision.

Viewing the said bungalow was not easy. It was in a dreadful state – the bath leaked and the floor was rotten. An elderly gentleman had lived there with a disabled wife. There were notches in all the doors where a wheelchair had been used, the kitchen was practically non-existent with a curtain under a butler sink, ring marks everywhere not wiped over, no cupboards, a walk-in pantry that was mucky. I don't think the occupant had updated the property in any way and the council had not. I thought the premises did have possibilities. It was on the end of a block of four. There were twelve properties in total, built for one person in the sixties. It was in a private estate of houses and the location was fine. A private car park alongside the bungalow and on the other side of the car park, four more bungalows.

I did not know how I could redo the property to my standard, but as always my daughter said she would help in any way she could. I tentatively wondered if the bank would give a small loan!

The only thing the council would do is re-emulsion the interior. The rest was up to me.

The small rear garden was a wilderness. The gentleman had grown vegetables and as happens in so many cases, advancing age, health problems, it had not been tended to for a long time. There were cabbage heads two feet high, a pond that was past its time and a breeding ground for flies, gnats and mosquitoes, that would definitely have to go.

I returned to my house, slept on it, talked at length to my daughter and two friends whose wisdom was always taken.

The next day, I went to the renting officer and said yes. This move I hoped would be the last and I hoped a turning point in my unstable life and I would feel more secure. My home had always been important to me and I wanted it to be again, even though it would never be truly my own, being council property.

I could not occupy the bungalow for a month. I did not mind, as I hoped I could do some work there, update the kitchen and the bathroom.

It was at this time, I found real help and friendship, which I will never forget.

One of my babysit friends offered to plan and go with me to a large DIY premises in the town to choose units etc. and also found a reliable plumber to install the bathroom suite. My lady I cleaned for gave me a very modern light for my kitchen and a lovely mirror and radiator for my bathroom. When I moved in, she gave me a microwave as a present.

My daughter, as always, gave me some money and I did go to the bank, with three letters of recommendation from my doctor, solicitor and a barrister. They interviewed me for an hour. I was honest and told them my circumstances and that I had two CCJs against me, for not being financially able to pay mortgage on my house and debts by my husband that had been proved not to be my fault, but which I was always being involved because I was a mortgagee and the person left to take the blame. Injustice in its highest form, I always felt, but could do nothing about.

After two days, the bank rang and granted me a loan, to be paid back in three years. The interest was phenomenal. That's banks isn't it?

If I reneged on the loan re. payments, they would take further action. I was able to buy the kitchen and bathroom, an oven, a fridge, and my daughter gave me a washing machine, which I paid her back later. I was very fortunate and life seemed much better.

I planned to organise the garden when I was in place. I intended to make it as low maintenance as possible. My arthritis was now very evident and no doubt would not improve, so I had to think ahead.

The council emulsioned everything standard magnolia and I was able to pick up the keys in mid-July and move in.

The first night, I was alone, I cried with relief and felt I did have some hope in my heart.

I got very good at trawling the charity shops, obtaining cutlery, two trays, two vases and bits and bobs one uses every day without thinking about it. I had my kitchen looking pristine in green and white. I think even my little dog felt at home at last. She loved to run around the garden, which was square in dimension. I inherited a round cushioned conifer and on one side of the garden I planted an Amelanchier tree suitable for small gardens, made a plan re. the design which had to come later when I had funds. Other than this, I felt very comfortable. The front overlook was great – a long front garden, grassed, cut by the council during the summer months. Across the road I looked onto a very well-manicured lawn and private houses. To the right, a row of immaculate cottages, painted white with slate roofs. To the right, a car park for residents and visitors for the occupants of the bungalows. There were only five cars belonging to residents, as most of the tenants were well over eighty and did not drive. There was a path running along the back of the bungalows and I noted I seemed to be the only resident who used my front entrance. On the side of my bungalow was, of course, the car park. I decided to plant Pyracantha, a prickly shrub, as I felt a little vulnerable as the access into my garden was very easy from the car park. On the other side, I had a lovely lady neighbour, whose married name and single name turned out to be the same as mine. She was such a clever lady, an excellent gardener – everything she put in the ground grew and flourished. She could build walls, service her car, there was nothing she could not do. Her garden was laid out like the village she grew up in and at Christmas people brought their children from far and wide to see the lights and Christmas decorations in her garden. There were about two thousand lights, Father Christmases, you name it, she lit it. All the proceeds went to Cancer Research and it was a very sad day for me when she died of cancer several years later, followed by a loyal and faithful daughter a year later. I put a little memorial stone in a bed near the car park, remembering her contribution to the village and all the good works she did.

The bungalow stood empty for six months.

My next neighbour was a nightmare. I'd rather not dwell on it. The police eventually dealt with it. They only stayed two years.

The present tenant is fine – very disabled, but helpful and kind, even though she has great disabilities.

In 2002, I felt settled in my little bungalow. Security for me would always be an issue, as the past years had taken their toll on many emotions. I have never felt really secure and resentment often looms re. my husband. I had got through anger, but resentment, I think, would always be in the corners of my mind. I missed being a couple, having someone to love and care for, discuss matters. I never felt lonely, just alone. I had only ever had one person in my life and there would never be another. I did and I still do, I only had love for one person and always in my mind, was trust. Without it no relationship can survive, at least not in my case. I shall always feel so betrayed and I could not, do not, want to feel that pain again. Everyone has pain when losing a partner. I always think it was not what my husband did, it was how he did it – always unfinished. A different type of grieving. Whenever I hear a favourite song, an anniversary, it still leaves a lump in my throat, a pain in my chest. It's grieving that never goes away. People say all kinds of words to help, but it just doesn't.

2003

A momentous year. I will recall.

I had been in my bungalow nearly two years. In March, one day, the post came and most of it was junk mail. One envelope did not look familiar. On opening it, it read To Whom It May Concern, asking who was managing my affairs, as the above had been notified I was deceased!

At first I thought it was a sick joke and I even laughed. There was a telephone number. I decided to telephone and see what it was all about.

I gave a reference and was again told I was deceased. I informed them this was not true, as I was speaking to them. I asked where this information had come from and they said it had come up on their computer. I thanked them and said I would be in touch in due course. I rang other relevant people – my two DDs, recipients and the Pensions Office. They all told me the same. I was mystified and concerned and did not know what to do. I telephoned my daughter, the C.A.B. and a wise friend I had met in the Victim Support.

Immediately I thought what was going to happen if I had no income. My friend suggested I wrote to the company who had initially sent the letter and explained that their information was untrue, sending a copy of my birth certificate and pension details. I heard nothing, not even an acknowledgement. This happened on a Thursday and I went as usual to collect my pension, only to be told it was not in place. I really began to feel panicky. I could not afford a solicitor and my lines of communication either by telephone or letter were not acknowledged. What was my next move? I decided I must somehow find the source of this wrong information.

Once again, I began to feel very insecure, as all the past events – losing my home, no finance – came into my mind. Panic attacks returned. I just could not lose this bungalow and have a nomad existence again. My daughter was propping me up again and the numerous explanations, which most people thought was funny, to me was very serious and unsettling.

I decided to go up to the head office in London to find out how this could happen. Letter writing and numerous phone calls, to no avail. I did not even receive an answer to my letters.

I made an appointment, hoping they had some authority and would be concerned re. my dilemma.

I took two letters of confirmation from my doctor and a barrister friend, saying I was alive and well, my birth certificate and numerous other paperwork, including the original letter advising me of my demise. I always photocopy letters etc. as I have no trust anymore re. businesses. I wonder sometimes how they conduct business and only come to life when there is money at the end of the process.

My appointment was 11:00 a.m. I was shown into a large, impressive office. No in or out trays, a telephone intercom, some plastic flowers, with an excellent view of London and the City. A middle aged gentleman followed me and showed a chair.

He appeared to listen intently to my account at what had happened. This took all of ten minutes. His only comment – he would look into the matter.

I stood my ground and said I was not leaving the office until I had two letters – one confirming I had not died and the other reinstating my accounts at the bank and other businesses who were not acknowledging the error made by themselves. Also, I did mention that whoever had fed this information in the computer should be reprimanded, as I pointed out, that if I had made same error, I would have been sacked and a letter from the Lord Chancellor telling me I was no longer a magistrate. He made no comment and left the room.

After what felt like an eternity, he returned with some paperwork! He informed me that an error had been made. A lady with my name and birth date had become deceased, but my name came into play. I did point out that his blame on the computer was all very well, but an employee had fed the information in and it should have been checked, even double-checked, if two names had been found. He gave me a letter explaining the situation and letters to my pension, direct debits etc.

I also asked that I wanted this information to be in operation within forty eight hours. It only meant pushing the right buttons – this time.

I told him if this did not happen, I would be in touch with an ombudsman, the newspapers etc. Also, I would take advice re. compensation for four and a half months of stress, incompetency and business conduct – not answering my correspondence (I always take copies) and their 'could not care less' approach to a serious matter. His only comment, I seemed a very determined lady. No apology, and I left the office.

This happened on a Wednesday. I'm more than glad to say, I checked everything on the following Friday. It appeared to be resolved. There followed another insult.

I went to a solicitors surgery, held in a hall near my home, once a month. They were appalled at my past situation. They fully recommended I ask for a settlement – approximately £500. One solicitor said £5,000, as the company concerned made that from interest rates per day, even in half a day.

I wrote to the gentleman I had seen before and who knew about the massive error they had made, asking for £500 compensation and at the same time there must be another family whose parent was deceased, were no doubt having great problems with probate and proving she was deceased!

One afternoon ten days later, I received a phone call from a young woman (would not give her name) who spoke to me as if she had a smell under her nose, asking me where had I plucked the amount of £500 from?

I asked politely if she had read my paperwork. There would be no need to ask that question.

After a great deal of what a wonderful company she worked for, she said she thought half that amount would be looked at – £35 was suggested and I should be grateful for that. I negotiated another £50 and called it a day. I just felt exhausted by the whole matter and did not want to hear their name again. I would like to add that when I asked to speak to the gentleman who interviewed me, I was told he was not available. I have noted on many occasions that when you do have a name, you are told they are on leave, have left the company, on holiday or have even died. We no longer have good communication skills and always passing the buck or even blame it on the computer! They knew my financial circumstances and that I received a cheque in due course with an acknowledgement slip. Great, don't you think reader?

More stress was not over and within four weeks, one of my direct debit companies made me bankrupt.

I could not take them to court, so I accepted.

Another blow, another challenge. I sometimes thought my husband had put a jinx on me.

This time it was disbelief. Evidently because I had not paid my loan of only £850, the company concerned said I had no financial means during the four months I had no income and although I had written and explained, they ignored and said this was the only way it could be resolved.

I had and knew no one who was made bankrupt and I did not know where to begin a defence.

I went to our local Crown Court to see what happens. Some people were very compassionate, others could not care less. I was advised to speak to the local bankruptcy office and ask for an interview.

All the people I had confronted over the past years, the gentleman in charge of my bankruptcy was the most understanding and could not comprehend how matters had become so stressful, through no fault of my own.

He decided to only make me bankrupt for fifteen months. He gave letters to present to the bank, explaining what had happened and recommended I was given a savings account and a current I paid into for my direct debit accounts, but I could not take money once I had paid it in. He also suggested a Post Office account, who did not seem to worry re. bankruptcy. I was relieved, as I honestly thought I would be struggling, like it happened when my husband left. Naturally, I had no credit rating and could not have any plastic. As I had lived okay without for many years, I was not worried, and he also said when my fifteen months were over he would personally have my name taken from the credit, so I would not be lumbered with that, which can be an ongoing problem.

When I left his office I could have danced for joy, if my arthritis had allowed. I was well pleased.

2004

I was now going into my seventy first year with high hopes. Surely nothing nasty could happen again?

The ladies' group I had joined on living in the village voted me as their chairlady, giving away to the idea that you have to live fifty years in a village before they accept you.

I enjoyed very much organising coach outings, for the first time since the group was formed, and we went to Slimbridge Wildlife, Highgrove House, Eden Experience, Rosemoor, and even a trip to London, which for some was a first not having ever left the Somerset County.

We met once a month, with various speakers and had a slap-up dinner every Christmas at a first class restaurant. I made a small gift for everyone, plus making friends. I stayed in the post for six years and thoroughly enjoyed. I only stood down as I felt another chair would have different ideas and a change is as good as a rest. The group has been disbanded, but twelve of us still belong to a coffee club and again meet once a month at a member's home.

My daughter and her husband had moved to Hastings – good for them, not for me, as the journey across country took well over four hours. My daughter commuted by road to London and I was apprehensive re. the journey in the winter, as it took approximately one and three quarter hours on B roads, and not good roads at that. They had bought an old house – not for me, as maintenance can be costly. They liked the space and garden and most of all the sea. Also a consideration, they had a large dog called 'Bob' and he had a ball, excuse the pun, playing on the beach and having a large garden to run around in.

The last stressful episode had really knocked my confidence again. For the second time I lost all trust and loyalty to any organisation. I felt I never was going to have some calm in my life, going from crisis to crisis.

One happy time happened later in the year. I had my first holiday since my husband had gone. It was all decided very quickly, not giving me time to worry about it.

My daughter telephoned and invited me to join them in Greece, a country I had only visited once before. Not feeling I wanted to be a gooseberry, I asked them if I could invite my cousin by marriage. The lady, now a widow, who my husband and I shared our house when we were first married. She jumped at the opportunity to accompany me, arranged the flights on the internet, flying from Gatwick to a destination I can't spell, but on the island of Lesvos.

My daughter and her husband would be already there taking a fortnight. We would spend their last week with them. What a week it was. Idyllic. We stayed in a Taverna right on the beach, run by a family who made us so welcome. Nothing was too much trouble.

My daughter and her husband would find their spot near some shade from wispy trees on the edge of the beach and my cousin and I had sun loungers on the seashore, reading and relaxing, going in for a swim whenever. I did not venture in the sea, as my arthritis was now very evident in my physique and I also had severe balance problems due to my ear condition. Nevertheless, we all had a great time, never a difference of opinion. My son-in-law was and is a very kind person and attended to every whim. We would dine under a canopy and me, in particular, would organise quizzes and charades. I'm sure my son-in-law groaned every time I started another quiz. He never said, as I know he would not want to upset me. My cousin was very impressed at his attentiveness, being a man among three ladies.

We often went into town, sat at cafés with a glass of wine, watching the world go by. I did not want it to end. He and my daughter were having a very stressful time at home, as his mother was terminally ill. A great strain on any relationship, but my son-in-law was a star and always there for his mother. She sadly died in January 2005.

In 2005, I was feeling once again that life was easier. I still wrote letters to my husband's two pension companies. Rarely did I even receive an acknowledgement and if I did, it was always the same. Due to the Data Protection Act, they could not help. I often wish a law was in place to protect the victim and I feel is ignored on most occasions. I always pointed out the Act did not apply if the person was deceased and would they let me know if that was the case – a fact most people are not aware of.

My daughter came down to see me. She wanted a serious talk with me. She felt I had held up so well from all the happenings in the last fourteen years. She asked me to try and put what had happened in a cobweb in my mind, as she felt I thought of nothing else and she wanted me to enjoy and have a quality of life. Reading between the lines, I had made it a burden for her as well. I respected her thoughts and admired her honesty and after a great deal of deliberation, knew she was right.

Since that time, we rarely speak of her dad and never re. his misdemeanours. I know she is hoping writing down all my thinking would be a healing process. I have reflected this over the last two years since I have been writing my thoughts down, but I feel it has not helped. I'm just glad it is nearly over. I started with a lot of enthusiasm, but it has not been sustained and I will, I hope, finish this manuscript up to date in 2013.

In 2006, I was bobbing along. I finished my cleaning job and my babysitting days were slowing down, as the children were all in their teens – most of them kept in touch. I always remembered their birthdays and Christmas.

A sad event for me. I had to have my little coffee-coloured poodle put to sleep. She was nearly fifteen, but was not well, on tablets for incontinence and I discovered a lump in her tummy. Any animal owner will know how awful it is to lose a faithful friend. I always feel it is your last gift to them to say farewell.

I talked myself into thinking she was my last dog which trebled my decision to have her put to sleep. I was now seventy three, maybe too old to have another dog. She was my seventh poodle and I missed her terribly. It is always great to come home to something alive and who needs you, and dogs are great levellers and a responsibility, other than yourself.

Also, my court work finished. I had been given three more years, as you usually have to retire at seventy. The police stepped in and requested I stay on, as I had so much experience and I was always asked for within the service. This also left a big void in my life. As they say, 'time marches on'. I find time a real enemy.

In the following years, things settled at last and although my credit was always in question, I had been awarded a disability pension which made life much easier.

A dear friend constantly told me to have another dog. My doctor also was insistent. Dogs give you unconditional love and my daughter assured me, if I did go ahead, she would not ever let me down if he needed re-homing. I held off for another year, when the same friend went to Crufts Dog Show, held in February in Birmingham, and spoke to several breeders there. A gentleman called Mr Storey said he was moving on four dogs, as he had recently had a heart bypass. He came highly recommended. She brought home photographs of two dogs and a bitch – Rupert, Tom and Alice. The only drawback was they were in Sheffield and I was in the West Country. I was lucky. My friend's husband insisted on taking me by car. The breeder sent me details and the following week, we left at 9:00 a.m. It seemed to take ages and we finally arrived at 1:00 p.m. I approached the house. Not a sound of any dogs. The breeder quickly came to the door. The house was immaculate, unusual as many breeders live higgledy-piggledy and in dog chaos. His wife met us and made tea and scones. Mr Storey asked me many questions about poodles and I had two references from my vet and another person, who had clipped my dogs over the last years.

Mr Storey said he would fetch the dogs. They were kept separately in kennels in the rear of the house. When they appeared, of course I was lost. They were lovely. Beautifully groomed and so well-behaved.

Mrs Storey only allowed them in the house in the evenings. Tom jumped on my lap, gave me lots of licks and I decided there and then he was the one for me. Mr Storey assured me I would not regret my decision and said he knew Tom was going to a loving home. I paid for him and we left and made the journey home. He was in a crate in the back and I made my friend stop twice, as Tom was so quiet I thought something had happened to him.

In hindsight, my only difference, I wish I had called him 'Sunny', as that is his character. He likes everyone and everyone likes him. My vet is his foster parent. He is glad he does not see him often, but when he does, he loves him. I really have a winner. He has been on a Universal calendar, won many rosettes. He is obedient to a fault, follows me everywhere, even waits outside when I'm in the loo. He has a tray full of soft toys and fetches them on command. As you can guess, I'm over the moon about him and so pleased I changed my mind and became a dog owner again. I guess as I have got older, I prefer dogs to people. They do not let you down in any way.

2008 was I call my medical year.

My arthritis was now very evident. I was told a new knee was inevitable and I thought I should get it done before I was much older, as you don't bounce back the older you become.

I tried to ignore the pain, but it was constant, and walking and driving were very difficult.

I decided to put the wheels in motion; doctor referral and waiting thirteen weeks for admission. I hoped it could be realised if I had it done in the autumn so that my recovery was in the early winter and I would be raring to go in the spring.

My cousin always said I could have a break in her second home by the sea in Cornwall and I really hoped to go in 2009 with a friend I had made through my Ménière's group.

If all went well I would be in hospital a week and providing I continued with my exercises, could return home.

I duly had my operation on a Thursday. All went well, although the pain level was very high and the exercises brought tears to my eyes. I was not allowed home until I had a ninety degree bend. I saw the consultant after six weeks. He was very pleased with my progress. I would think twice about the other leg.

Two years later I had to have another ear operation. I do walk without pain and that is the most important issue. I was told it takes a good year to make a full recovery.

Enough of my woe.

My life had settled down. I enjoyed my little bungalow. My garden was low maintenance. I was disappointed that village life was not a challenge. There was little enthusiasm and spontaneity. I liked living in a beautiful county, but always got a buzz when I went to the capital and I sometimes wished I had been able to move back to Surrey after my husband left. It is too late now, of course. I could not sustain it financially and I felt I had had enough upheaval to last a lifetime.

I still wrote a letter every year to my husband's private pension company. I have received two letters in twenty years, always the same answer, due to the Data Protection Act, no information would be forthcoming. I wish there was an act that protected victims! There must be thousands like myself, ordinarily good people who are plagued in the same way, and I feel that although I am a small voice, you have to start somewhere. The only thing that brings change is people power. Besides, the general public are unaware the Data Protection Act does not cover people who are deceased and as time marches on, my husband will be eighty two this year, 2013. Things could be altered and at least it would bring closure to unfinished business and so much heartache.

2010

Yet another year with an unpleasant event, this time to Tom, my dog.

I collect every year for Cancer Research. I usually do it in three days, spending an afternoon doing different parts of the village. On this particular day, I was doing the collecting on my last day. It is surprising how the public behave and a real eye-opener. I was on the last lap, with Tom beside me, on a lead of course. I approached a bungalow. There were no gates. I entered the porch and rang the bell. I could hear the occupant coming to the door. On opening, two dogs rushed past, grabbed Tom, dragged him across the lawn. One dog stood over him and the other started biting him. Three small children looking on and now the owner with her partner, standing in the doorway, doing nothing.

I ran over and hit the biting dog with my collecting tin and grabbed Tom who was not moving, but making yelps and screams and I ran into the open garage. The dogs, two Staffordshire Bull Terriers, followed me. I was holding Tom aloft and they were biting my legs and clothes. After a few minutes the owner called them in and said it is not as bad as it looks and went indoors. I was in shock and called to them that I wanted to go to the vet, as dogs can die from shock and Tom was bleeding from a gaping hole in the soft part of the mouth and lip. His ear was torn badly and there was a gash very close to his eye. His back left leg was just hanging at a different angle. I was so frightened. My clothes were covered in blood and all I could think of was my good dog was in a very sorry state. After what seemed an eternity, the lady of the house ushered me to the car and we proceeded the three mile journey to our vet. I was seen right away. By this time Tom was very quiet. His eyes were closed and he was violently shaking. The vet very efficiently gave him an injection and then asked me questions whilst at the same time feeling Tom's limp body. He had sustained several bites, his ear was badly torn and needed stitching and his other wounds, it was explained, could not be stitched as there may be bacteria within the bite and hopefully would heal themselves. He had another injection of antibiotic and the vet wanted to see him the following day. Quietly but firmly he told the owner of the fighting dogs, they should be muzzled and a warning sign on the front door or porch. He also asked if this had happened before. She was non-committal. I learnt afterwards it had, on several occasions, and I added she should realise how dangerous they could be to her young children. I remarked your children are paramount and time will tell. Six months later, I learned the dog, the more vicious of the two, had been destroyed as it had bitten a small boy's face!

I did not speak on our way home and I asked her if she would return my collecting box which was still in their garden. She was not very forthcoming on the journey. No apology and I was glad to be in my own home.

I have never been on that road since this happening.

Two days later Tom developed kidney failure. The vet gave me the prognosis. It could be very serious and he hoped it was only a shock reaction. He immediately went on medication. The vet suggested the expense should be with the owners of the dogs. She had paid the initial bill of over £153. I was so concerned, I did not worry re. the expenses. I would sell something if I had to.

The following fortnight Tom was monitored every day and after five weeks, showed signs of improvement and after three months, the vet was pleased to tell me he would recover fully.

One evening four weeks later, there was a knock on my door and the owner of the said dogs threw the bill in my porch and said no way were they paying, told me I was a stupid dog owner and I should not bring my dog on private property etc. I told him he was a bully like his dogs, but I was very upset. They never came around to ask about Tom's welfare or mine. I found out this was a solicitor (the lady of the said dogs). I do not intend to elaborate, to me, it just shows how unkind and unsympathetic people are.

I used to be very honoured to live in this country which I love, but as I have become older, and I think wiser, I am disenchanted and very disappointed that most people, not all, are uncaring, ill-mannered and all they think of is themselves.

So many good things are no longer there. Greed is at the helm most of the time and I find it very worrying our values are in jeopardy and our character frail and non-existent.

I still collect for Cancer Research, but have never been in that road again.

Other than this very unpleasant event, 2010 came and went.

I had a lovely week in Cornwall with my friend.

Tom had a great time playing with other dogs on the beach. I was always anxious – perhaps dogs, unlike elephants, don't have good memories. I would refute this as a friend of mine had to leave her dog to live abroad. She returned two years later and her dog, once he heard her voice, it was as if she had never been away.

2011

A very bad winter. On one occasion I did not go out for fourteen days and when I did, I had a bad fall, broke two ribs and had a hairline fracture on my spine. I had to be very wary of walking and I was always aware of my knee as I now had developed osteoporosis and falling could be a real hazard.

Once again my friend and I went to Cornwall in early May. The weather was good and we lazed around, went to Padstow and bought pasties, went to a National Trust inland, I cannot pronounce the name, so therefore cannot write it. My friend is great company and always kind. She is fifteen years younger than me, but have interests the same and we always love visiting gardens.

My daughter and her husband were seriously thinking of moving. My daughter was finding the commute to London and the zoning and parking so stressful, especially in the winter. Their Victorian house always costing money. They were not very optimistic re. moving to London. Prices were rocketing, a severe recession was now happening since the bank crisis. It brought to my mind, once again, the minister expenses scandal and how few were prosecuted. If I had taken money under false pretences, I would have no doubt gone to jail! Remembering my deceased episode, when through no fault of my own, I was made bankrupt...

In October, they viewed a twelve year old mews house in Penge, SE20. They liked it very much. It was near enough to the Capital and had an almost village feel with all the extras – shopping, open spaces, Crystal Palace Park – and many other good features. They put their house on the market and it was duly sold to an Indian gentleman and his family. They had hoped to move after Christmas, but one never knows how the wheels turn and they moved in a week before Christmas.

Christmas for them was chaotic, but they were happy and I think it is the best house they have lived in. They are putting their stamp on it and I hope they will be happy there. I hope they have got Victoriana out of their system and can enjoy without any hassle.

My daughter loves it, as there is no hassle re. parking. It's warm, a garden they can deal with. My daughter is the gardener and plants tomatoes, peppers, courgettes, and always has flowers in her home.

The big plus is I can now see her more often as the journey across country was not easy and very expensive.

Here we are. My writing will soon be over.

In 2012 I visited my daughter, endured like everyone else a dreadful rainy spring, summer and autumn. The village was cut off as we are on a severe flood plain. Fortunately, and it is more than fortunate, my bungalow is situated up a grassy bank, but the four bungalows on the other side had to be evacuated and their homes were so badly flooded, they had to vacate for repairs to wiring and decoration.

I have forgotten to mention previously that in October 2000 we were in flood, three months after I moved in. I lost my car which floated out of the car park and was only salvaged as there was too much damage, as it was overwhelmed with water. Two other neighbours' cars had the same fate.

To add to my continuing bad luck, in late January 2012 I had a very bad car accident.

I was returning from delivering a gift to a friend in the next village. As I left her road, I felt the car shift, as if the whole car was, I felt, not in control. I was doing approximately thirty five miles an hour, going downhill, towards a one-way bridge over the Tone River. I decided to bypass the river crossing in case I could not steer the car properly. I had my foot on the brake, nothing was happening. As I took a side road, that I had never been down before, my car was now doing fifty to sixty miles an hour and was out of control. I applied the handbrake – it sheared off at the base and as I dangerously went round a bend, in the opposite direction a 4X4 Range Rover hit me head on. My safety bag did not blow and the bar on the Range Rover came into my car and it was twelve inches in front of me.

I don't know whether it was fortunate or not, but the 4X4 was driven by two retired policemen. The most frightening thing, I could not get out, as the chassis had just collapsed. I had to be cut out of my motor and the whole of the front had caved in. I was very frightened and panicky, afraid the car would catch fire. I was taken to hospital with many injuries – a fractured collar bone, five broken ribs, a fractured pelvis – and I was told by the hospital how fortunate I was. If I had taken the route over the bridge and met another vehicle, I would have been in the river, which does not bear thinking about. My left hand was badly damaged and I had to have two knuckles removed and pins and plates inserted, and of course I could no longer hold the wheel of a car.

I gradually recovered. My ribs were so painful, more than anything. I decided I was recovering physically, but emotionally I had lost confidence and I gave up – fifty years' driving without ever having an accident. I felt it was time. Not to worry about insurance, maintenance and the stress of driving on the roads today. I would have had to have the car revamped due to my hand injury and just felt I would call it a day.

I do count my blessings. My doctor arranged free transport through Social Services. I had a carer who did my shopping and if she is not available, I ring in my groceries and they are delivered. Also my prescriptions are delivered and I have two true friends who will help when needed. I had compensation this time with no questions as to why and where. They took my car to the factory, all done on computers I believe. They found I had complete brake failure and other verbal explanations as to the mechanics. They offered me a new car or money. I, of course, took the latter and for the first time in twenty one years I had some money in the bank.

Perhaps I was getting a green light at last.

I also had a great holiday with my daughter. We went to a hotel in Berkshire. It was lovely to have my girlie all to myself. I had reservations re. the venue as it is for adults only and nearly all over sixty five plus, but she communicates well and gets a lot of generation information and respects senior citizens. We hoped we would go again next year, to a different locality.

2013

I celebrated my eightieth birthday with my daughter and son-in-law, balloons, cake, and a super dinner. I stayed a week. We went out a great deal and celebrated every day. I have always had a 'thing' about my birth date. It is so near New Year. There is no post on the actual date. People include it in their Christmas cards or just overlook it. I always say, my parents in their time of passion did not give a thought to my birthday. Nevertheless, I'm glad I'm here and I had wonderful parents.

So many children no longer have this privilege, which is both distressing and sad for all concerned, but particularly children.

It was a long and severe winter. Plans were made for Cornwall once again with my friend. We were going in early June. My friend had moved into the nearby town and we saw each other often.

Our holiday was the beginning of a very warm summer. We deserved it. We can never depend on the weather and it's a long time to wait, with our grey days and rain. At least, I always think, we can go out on most days in this country and don't have any extremes.

My daughter and I are going away again in middle September, this time to Herefordshire. We are hoping to visit Gloucester Cathedral and two other days can be booked, Tewkesbury and Ledbury.

I have lived here thirteen years. I feel very comfortable, miss the buzz of town living. I will never be wholly a country girl, due of course to my upbringing.

I cannot believe I have been on my own over twenty two years, more than half the time I was married.

My husband is never far from my thoughts. I am resigned to never seeing him again, never hearing his voice or feeling good in his presence.

My only bewilderment is the young, caring, loving man I married went away, never caring what would happen to me and never seeing his daughter again.

I do not think he was a bad person. He did not have the strength of character and events festered in his mind – his start in life, the fire of his thriving business, the Post Office episode on the Isle of Wight – when things started going wrong, he took a coward's way out and ran away, and just did not care about the people who loved him the most. I think it is due to my daughter and our endurance and fortitude that has got us through very dark times. Without my girlie, I too may not have made it. My doctor said to me at the outset, you have two choices – sink or swim, and I think you are a good swimmer. I knew I could not let my daughter down like her father and I hope I have fulfilled that wish to myself, and to her. It is awful to love someone and they no longer love or care about you. It hurts like crazy.

VALERIE MAY

I am always wondering about my husband.
I wonder what he has done with his life in the last twenty plus years.
I wonder if he ever thinks of me, or his daughter.
I wonder if he regrets his actions.
I wonder if he is still here.
I'm always wondering – there is no ending.

Summary

I used my kitchen worktop to write this manuscript as I do not have a table in my small bungalow. It took just over two years.

I hope the reader will read the emphasis on injustice. You read in the newspapers and hear on the news every week, re. injustice. My experiences have, of course, been my reasons to bringing it to the fore.

So many of our laws no longer apply. They need to be reviewed and changed to involve what happens in present day society which has changed dramatically over the last twenty five years. Also, sentencing. You get a longer prison sentence robbing a bank than taking someone's life. Life does not mean life. It's farcical to have a shorter sentence after so many years, when murder is the foremost issue.

Also, I hope you will see how money comes to the top of the list. It speaks all languages.

I'm sure if a male had experienced the inclusions I have, they too would have been addressed in a different way. Men and women are still treated in a sexist manner and very little compassion is evident. My husband was considered a 'bit of a lad' and even admired, always by men. If I had behaved in that way, I would have been called a 'scarlet woman'. or worthless.

Postscript: 2016

When I finished my book in 2012, as stated on the first page, there was no ending.

In November 2014 I heard by letter from my husband's pension company – I had always kept in touch over the years. My husband died in October 2013 in a public hospital in New South Wales Australia.

I wrote to the public records office in New South Wales, and after mountains of red tape and five months later, asking questions like "why do you want a death certificate?", and again showing no empathy or understanding of my situation, that I had lived with for twenty four years.

I was deeply saddened, but also relieved that he could not hurt me or our daughter anymore.

His death certificate did not acknowledge me or our daughter and every question asked was answered "unknown".

So I do have closure to my true story at last.

A foolish and dishonourable man.

Made in the USA
Columbia, SC
17 January 2018